SAMS
Teach Your

C000060500

Windows® 98

by Jennifer Fulton

in 10 Minutes

SAMS

A Division of Macmillan Computer Publishing
201 West 103rd St., Indianapolis, Indiana 46290 USA

To my little angle, Katerina.

Copyright ©1998 Sams® Publishing

Library of Congress Catalog No.: 98-84769

ISBN: 0-672-31330-8

01 00 99 98   4 3

Interpretation of the printing code: the rightmost double-digit number is the year of the book's printing; the rightmost single-digit number, the number of the book's printing. For example, a printing code of 98-1 shows that the first printing of the book occurred in 1998.

Screen reproductions in this book were created using Collage Plus from Inner Media, Inc., Hollis, NH.

Executive Editor Grace Buechlein
Acquisitions Editor Stephanie McComb
Technical Editors Craig Arnush, Christie Gleeson
Managing Editor Sarah Kearns
Copy Editors Keith Cline, Gayle Johnson, Daryl Kessler, Amy Lepore
Indexer Christine Nelsen
Cover Designer Aren Howell
Book Designer Gary Adair
Production Team Becky Stutzman, Pamela Woolf

ABOUT THE AUTHOR

Jennifer Fulton is a computer trainer, consultant, and best-selling author of over 50 books covering many areas of computing, including DOS, Windows 3.1, Windows 95, and Windows 98. Jennifer is a self-taught veteran of computing, which means that if something can happen to a computer user, it has happened to her at one time or another. As a computer veteran, Jennifer brings what's left of her sense of humor to her many books, including: *Big Basics Book of Windows 95, Netscape Navigator 6 in 1, Ten Minute Guide to Excel 97, Big Basics Book of Office 97, Easy Outlook, Big Basics Book of PCs, Computers: A Visual Encyclopedia, 20th Century Computers,* and *How They Worked (The Official Starfleet History of Computers).* Jennifer began her writing career as a staff writer for Alpha Books, a former division of Macmillan Computer Publishing, before escaping to the life of a freelance author. Jennifer lives in Indianapolis with her husband, Scott, who is also a computer book author. They live together in a small home filled with many books, some of which they have not written.

ACKNOWLEDGMENTS

I would like to thank everyone for their involvement in this project, including Acquisitions Editor Stephanie McComb, Development Editor Philip Wescott, and Copy Editor Gayle Johnson. I appreciate the opportunity to write for Sams and to collaborate once again with the great people who work there.

WE'D LIKE TO HEAR FROM YOU!

As part of our continuing effort to produce books of the highest possible quality, MCP would like to hear your comments. To stay competitive, we really want you, as a computer book reader and user, to let us know what you like or dislike most about this book or other Macmillan products.

You can send comments, ideas, or suggestions for improving future editions to us at **operating systems.mcp.com**. The address of our Internet site is **http://www.mcp.com** (World Wide Web).

Thanks in advance—your comments help us to continue publishing the best books available on computer topics in today's market.

Although we cannot provide general technical support, we're happy to help you resolve problems you encounter related to our books, disks, or other products. If you need such assistance, please contact our Tech Support department at 800-545-5914 ext. 3833.

CONTENTS

INTRODUCTION

WHAT'S NEW IN WINDOWS 98

Windows is the world's most popular operating system, and one reason for this is its graphical user interface (GUI). Windows lets users issue commands by clicking icons and work with programs within easily manipulated screens called (appropriately) *windows*.

 Operating System The operating system lets your computer interpret requests from applications and commands from you, the user. The operating system is the "brain" of your PC, enabling it to manage data.

Windows 98 represents the marriage of the Windows operating system and Internet access. This unique melding of form and function, known as *Web integration,* helps you perform routine computer tasks such as writing a letter while maintaining seamless access to the information you need from the Internet. Web integration also changes the way you interact with the Windows operating system. Command and navigation procedures, as well as the look of the Windows 98 interface, all more closely resemble their counterparts on the Web.

 Internet The Internet is a worldwide network of computers originally designed by the U.S. government to protect the national defense. Today, the Internet is used by universities, corporations, government offices, and private individuals. The Internet uses a common protocol (language) that allows these vastly different networks to share information.

Intranet This is a company-wide network that uses the same protocols as the Internet to provide mainly internal access to company documents and other information.

World Wide Web   This is called the Web or the WWW for short. Unlike most other parts of the Internet, which are text-based, the Web displays data in a graphical format on *Web pages*. Web pages are linked like a vast spider web—hence the name.

For example, you can set up your Desktop to actively receive updates from your favorite Web sites, such as stock information, news updates, and the like. You can also receive automatic updates from your company's local intranet.

In addition, Windows 98 lets you manage your files and the folders that contain them using the methodology of the Internet and the World Wide Web. For example, you can now open a program with a single-click of the mouse instead of double-clicking, as you might in Windows 3.1 or Windows 95. This is similar to the method you use to play a sound file on a Web page. You can also enter the location of files into Windows 98's file management program using the same addressing technique that's used on the Internet. Once you learn one file management system, there's nothing new to learn.

As an option, the icons that represent Windows 98 files can be displayed within Weblike pages, with their own graphical layout and design, making it simpler for you to locate and identify files and applications and ascertain their purposes. For example, your local system administrator could design a page that contains links to various files on your local network, complete with descriptions of their contents and use.

 Compatibility Issues   Windows 98 will run both 16-bit applications (Windows 3.1) and 32-bit applications (Windows 95 and 98). So any program you might already be using on these older versions of Windows is compatible with Windows 98.

In short, Windows 98 offers you these advantages:

- **Performance improvements**, such as faster performance and load times, improved Plug and Play hardware detection, and improved power management.

- **Configuration improvements**, such as display setting enhancements and the new Accessibility Settings Wizard.

- **An improved help system** that includes integrated online help and automated system updates.

- **New utilities** such as the Maintenance Wizard, Fat 32 Converter, and System File Checker. In addition, old standbys such as the Backup and ScanDisk utilities have been greatly improved.

- **Cool multimedia features** such as broadcast services that bring your TV to your Desktop, an imaging tool that lets you easily view any graphic file, and multiple display support.

- **New Internet/communication tools**, including the Connection Wizard, Internet Explorer 4.0, Outlook Express, FrontPage Express, NetMeeting, and built-in setup for online services such as America Online.

How to Use This Book

This book is designed for the reader who doesn't have a lot of time to learn about a new program or, in this case, a new operating system. Each lesson in this book is designed to take only 10 minutes to complete. So even in a busy workday, you can still find the time to learn what you need.

You can informally divide this book into four sections. The first seven lessons concentrate on general Windows 98 features, including lessons on the organization of the Windows 98 desktop, the Active Desktop, windows and dialog boxes you find in each Windows program, and Windows 98 Help. The next seven lessons deal with customizing Windows 98 and file and directory management. After that, the next nine lessons deal with the general operation of Windows and DOS applications, as well as the accessory programs that are provided as part of the Windows 98 package, and printing and disk management with Windows 98. The final five lessons present network-related features of the operating system, such as the use of Internet Explorer as a Web browser, the management of electronic mail services, and the use of Network Neighborhood. This book also includes appendixes on configuring a modem and other hardware settings and configuring for the Internet or an online service.

You should probably complete the lessons in order, but you can feel free to skip around after you complete Lesson 7.

CONVENTIONS USED IN THIS BOOK

This book uses the following conventions:

- Information you type appears in **boldface** type.
- Menus and menu options, dialog box options, keys you press, and names of buttons and dialog box tabs appear in color type.

When instructing you to choose menu commands, I use two different formats. Shorter menu options look something like this: "From the File menu, choose Open." Longer menu options look something like this: "Click Start, and then select Programs | Accessories | Communications | Phone Dialer." The vertical bar (|) could be considered a substitute for the words "and then select."

In addition to these conventions, this book uses the following sidebars to identify helpful information:

 Tips point out shortcuts and solutions that can save you time and energy.

 Cautions help you avoid common pitfalls.

 Plain English explains new terms and definitions.

INTRODUCING WINDOWS 98

*In this lesson, you'll learn how to start
and shut down Windows 98. You will
also learn how to use the mouse (including
how to use the Microsoft IntelliMouse) and the Windows Start button.*

STARTING WINDOWS 98

Windows 98 should start automatically every time you turn on
your computer. When Windows 98 starts it prepares your computer for use, a process called *booting* the computer.

Next you'll see a log on dialog box. This dialog box contains either
two or three text boxes. The User Name box should already contain
your name or the name under which your computer is presently
registered. The box marked Domain, if it's there, should also be
filled in already with the name of the domain your system administrator wants you to use. The box marked Password should be
blank, except for a blinking cursor. Type your password and press
Enter. (If you are part of a network and don't know what your password is, consult your network system administrator.) As you type,
Windows inserts asterisks into the Password box. These aren't the
characters you're actually typing—they just represent the fact that
you are typing characters, in case anyone is peeking over your
shoulder.

Remember That Password You must know your password to access a network using Windows 98. If you don't
log on to Windows 98 with your password, you won't have
access to any local area network (LAN) that might be
available. However, if you really need to get into Windows
98, but you don't need to be on the network, you can
press Esc when you see the log on dialog box.

I See a Startup Menu If you are first prompted with a numbered menu with the header "Windows 98 Startup Menu," instead of the log on dialog box, you are either being asked to choose from one of several configurations your system administrator has set up for you, or something peculiar may have happened the last time you tried to shut down Windows 98. Contact your administrator, if you have one, to find out which number you should choose in this instance. Otherwise, you should probably just pick the Normal option to boot as if nothing out of the ordinary happened. Most Windows 98 users won't see this menu.

In a moment you'll see the Welcome to Windows 98 dialog box. This dialog box gives you the opportunity to register your copy of Windows 98 with Microsoft, connect to the Internet, tour Windows 98 features, or run maintenance tasks on your Windows 98 system. If you don't want this dialog box to appear each time you start Windows 98, you can "deselect" the check box in the lower-left corner of the dialog box. (You can always access it again by selecting Start | Programs | Accessories | System Tools | Welcome to Windows.) To close the box, use the mouse to click on the Close button (the × in the upper-right corner of the box.) (If you are unfamiliar with using a mouse, you may want to skip ahead to the "Using the Mouse" section in this lesson and read it now.)

In a few moments, you'll see the Windows 98 Desktop, which should appear similar (although perhaps not identical) to Figure 1.1. The term *Desktop* is used metaphorically here. It symbolizes how the objects you work with in Windows are arranged and managed, like the papers and other objects on your desk in the real world.

 The Other Desktop Windows 98 offers you a choice of two different Desktops: the Classic Desktop and the Active Desktop. You'll learn more about the Active Desktop and how to switch between it and the Classic Desktop in Lesson 2, "Navigating the Windows 98 Desktop."

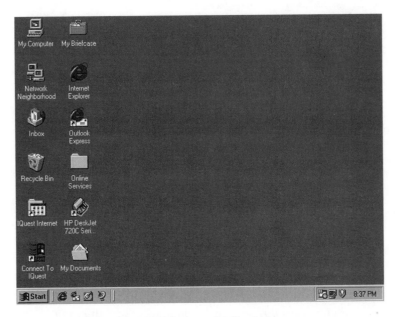

FIGURE 1.1   The Classic Windows 98 Desktop.

USING THE MOUSE

A *mouse* is a device that you use to manipulate objects in Windows. As you move the mouse on its pad, the mouse pointer onscreen moves in tandem. The *mouse pointer,* or simply *pointer,* is the small symbol (such as an arrow) that moves on the screen when you move the mouse.

Since the mouse is such a simple device, mechanically speaking, there are only a few gestures you'll ever need to perform with it:

- To *point* to an object on the screen, move the mouse pointer directly over that object. You point to an object when you are preparing to do something to it.

- To *click* an object to which your mouse pointer is currently pointing, you press the left mouse button once and quickly release it. Generally, you click an object to issue a command, open a program, or select an object.

- To *right-click* an object, point to it and then press and release the right mouse button. When you right-click an object, Windows and many applications display a menu called a *context menu,* which lists commands that pertain to that object.

- To *drag* an object from place to place, you first point to it and then click and hold down the mouse button—don't release it yet. Next, you move the pointer in the direction you want to drag the object. When the pointer is in the position where you want the object to appear, you release the mouse button. (If you want to drag a word or paragraph, you have to *select* it first.) The process of dragging an object to a new place is called *drag and drop.* You might use drag and drop to move a file from one directory to another or to move a paragraph within a word processing document. Normally a drag operation involves the left mouse button; however, Windows 98 and some Windows programs employ so-called *right-drags* (using the right mouse button) that bring up a context menu after the button is released.

- To *double-click* an object, you point to it and then press and release the left mouse button twice rapidly. Double-clicking is the standard method in Windows for starting an application or selecting an object from a dialog box and immediately closing the box (dismissing it).

Too Slow or Too Fast? If you're having trouble clicking and double-clicking with the mouse, you might want to adjust its speed. See Lesson 8, "Customizing Windows 98," for help. If you are not accustomed to using a mouse, a good way to practice is to play one of the games that come with Windows 98. You can find the games on the Start menu under Programs | Accessories | Games. See Figure 1.2.

How Using the Mouse Is Different in Web Style

When you turn on Windows 98's new Web Style option, the way your mouse operates changes dramatically. For instance, to select an object, instead of clicking once on that object with the left mouse button, you point to it, stop the mouse completely, and wait for Windows to recognize that the pointer has stopped (about a third of a second by default). Windows will then highlight the object you selected.

Also, double-clicking is replaced entirely with single-clicking, thus treating each object as though it were a hyperlink. With the Web Style option turned on you can simply click a file to open it. The optional Web Style setting is covered in greater detail in Lesson 10, "Drive, Folder, and File Management Options" and Lesson 11, "Viewing Drives, Folders, and Files."

Using the IntelliMouse

Because Microsoft is the manufacturer of both Windows 98 and the IntelliMouse pointer device, Microsoft has naturally provided extra support for the IntelliMouse. This Microsoft-brand pointer has a small, gray, vertical wheel between its two buttons. This wheel is used for scrolling, and it can also be clicked—to act as a third button of sorts.

Windows applications that can work with the IntelliMouse driver (especially Microsoft-brand software) can make use of the IntelliMouse wheel. Here are the basics:

- To scroll slowly, rotate the wheel up or down.

- To scroll more quickly, click the wheel once and then move the mouse in the direction in which you want to scroll. Click the wheel again to turn off the automatic scrolling.

- To zoom in or out, press the Ctrl key as you rotate the wheel up (to zoom in) or down (to zoom out).

For instance, with Microsoft Excel 97, you can use the wheel to *pan* through a worksheet the way a camera pans a scene by rotating the wheel. Using the wheel more like a button, you can hold it down and then move the mouse in the direction you want to scroll. Or you can press the Ctrl key while rotating the wheel up or down to increase or decrease, respectively, the "zoom" factor of the active worksheet.

Using the Start Button

Almost every operation you initiate in Windows 98 begins with the Start button, located in the lower-left corner of the screen. You can start programs, change Windows features, locate files, shut down Windows, and perform other operations with the commands you'll find on the Start menu, as shown in Figure 1.2.

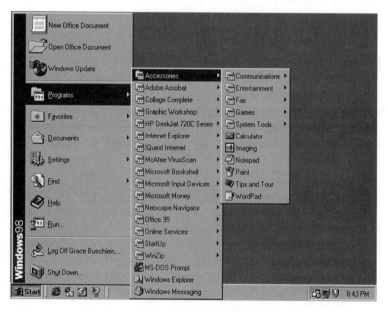

Figure 1.2 The Start menu, which is displayed when you click the Start button.

When you click the Start button, the Start menu appears. Here are brief descriptions of the commands that are displayed:

- If you have a connection to the Internet, you can use the Windows Update command to update your version of Windows periodically. This command connects you to the Microsoft Web site.

- Programs displays a categorized listing of the applications (programs) available on your system. Navigate through the various categories or *submenus* that appear until you find the program you intend to start.

- Favorites brings up a list of the documents, channels, and Internet links you have previously selected for convenient access from this command.

- Documents displays a list of documents that have recently been accessed or created with your applications. You can click one of these entries to open the document in the associated application.

- Settings displays a short list where you can access, among other things, the Control Panel. In the Control Panel you can change the major characteristics of the operating system, such as display properties, printer status, and computer setup.

- Find helps you locate files, folders, or computers on your system or on your company's network. You can also use Find to locate Web pages on the Internet, or people's email addresses.

- Help brings up the Windows 98 Help system, which provides information on the various aspects of Windows 98, including quick pointers on using the operating system.

- Run lets you enter a program's executable filename, either by typing it in or by browsing for it in your file directories. One case in which you might use the Run command is to initiate the setup command for a new software program.

- Log Off lets you log off your company's network and log back on under a different user profile (a set of customized configuration settings). You might use this command when you share your computer with a coworker.

- Shut Down provides the means for shutting down Windows safely. You can also use this command to restart (*reboot*) your computer when needed.

As you select commands from some parts of the Start menu, additional menus are displayed. For example, when you select Programs a listing of the programs installed on your computer and your program groups, are displayed.

SHUTTING DOWN WINDOWS 98

When it is time for you to turn your computer off, don't just flip the Off switch. Doing so might damage your computer files. You need to shut down Windows 98 first and then let the system tell you when it's okay to flip the Off switch. To shut down Windows 98 and prepare to turn off your machine, do the following:

1. Close all your open applications, making sure that any documents you're currently working on are saved.

2. Click the Start button.

3. From the Start menu, select Shut Down. Windows displays the dialog box shown in Figure 1.3.

FIGURE 1.3   The Shut Down Windows dialog box.

4. Make sure that the Shut down choice is selected, and then click OK. Windows initiates its shut-down procedure and soon informs you that it is safe to turn off your computer.

 Please Stand By   Some computers let you suspend their operations, which means to switch them into low-power mode, maintaining just the central processor without the peripherals, hard drive, or display. The Power Management options in Windows allow you to maintain what you're currently doing on your computer with the minimum amount of power necessary. Using the Power Management options is an alternative to shutting down your computer and restarting your programs from scratch when you want to work again. If your computer supports *standby mode*, the Stand By command will appear just above Shut Down on the Start menu. For more information on Power Management, see Lesson 8, "Customizing the Appearance of Windows 98."

OTHER SHUT-DOWN OPTIONS

The Shut Down menu provides additional options. Here's when to use them:

Restart: You might need to restart your computer after making a system configuration change (such as changing the screen resolution), or to refresh Windows' internal resources. You'll find that running multiple applications at once often causes a severe drain on your system's resources. By restarting your PC, you can remove all programs from memory and refresh your system.

 The Old Ctrl+Al+Delete   In the early days of PCs, users restarted their PCs by pressing Ctrl+Alt+Delete. This "three-finger salute" is used in Windows 98 to bring up a dialog box that lets you close a program (end a task) without shutting down the entire system, or to initiate an emergency shut-down when your system locks up.

Restart in MS-DOS mode: Programs written for the MS-DOS operating system will most likely run in Windows 98 without your having to switch to "MS-DOS mode." Many DOS programs are displayed in their own windows and won't interfere with other Windows functions or applications. However, some "legacy" applications (programs that were originally created for use on an earlier operating system, such as MS-DOS), especially graphically intense games, require you to shut down "Windows mode" in order to eliminate the constraints that Windows places on running programs.

 Don't Just Shut Down   While in MS-DOS mode, don't shut down your computer by just turning it off. Instead, when you're ready to turn off your computer, first return to Windows mode by typing **exit** at the command prompt and pressing Enter. Windows responds with the message Windows is now restarting. Soon the entire operating system will be restarted. From there, you can initiate the regular Windows shutdown procedure outlined earlier.

LOGGING ON AS A DIFFERENT USER

Windows 98 allows multiple users to share the same computer while maintaining the individual preferences of each user. This is accomplished by setting up passwords for each user and having each user enter his password, thus *logging on,* when Windows 98 is started. Logging on also affects your network connection—meaning that you will be logged off the network and then logged back on as a different user when you follow this procedure.

By the way, logging on again doesn't require a complete shutdown of the system, but it will close all running applications—so make sure you save your work and shut down your programs before proceeding. To log on as a different user, follow these steps:

1. Click the Start button.

2. From the Start menu, select Log Off, as shown in Figure 1.4.

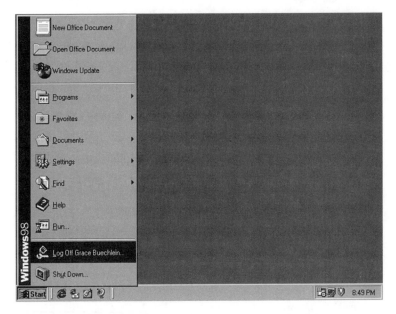

FIGURE 1.4   Logging off

3. Click Yes. The Welcome to Windows dialog box appears.

4. Enter the User name and Password you want to use, and then click OK.

In this lesson, you learned about the major components of the Windows 98 Desktop and how the mouse is used to manipulate those components. You also saw how to start, restart, and shut down Windows 98. In the next lesson, you'll learn the difference between the Classic and the Active Desktops, along with how to use the taskbar and the toolbars.

2 NAVIGATING THE WINDOWS 98 DESKTOP

In this lesson, you'll learn how to turn on the Active Desktop and how to switch back to the Classic Desktop when needed. You'll also learn how to use the Windows taskbar and the toolbars.

UNDERSTANDING THE WINDOWS 98 DESKTOP

The Windows 98 Desktop appears when you start Windows. The Desktop holds objects, shown as *icons,* that you use to start applications; copy, move, and delete files; connect to the Internet; and perform other functions. The Classic Windows Desktop is shown in Figure 2.1. You'll learn how to use the Desktop components later in this lesson.

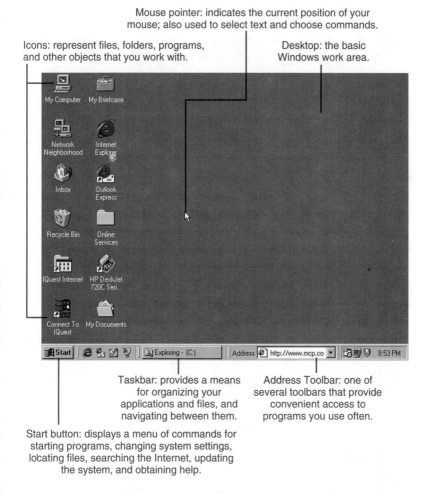

Mouse pointer: indicates the current position of your mouse; also used to select text and choose commands.

Icons: represent files, folders, programs, and other objects that you work with.

Desktop: the basic Windows work area.

Taskbar: provides a means for organizing your applications and files, and navigating between them.

Address Toolbar: one of several toolbars that provide convenient access to programs you use often.

Start button: displays a menu of commands for starting programs, changing system settings, locating files, searching the Internet, updating the system, and obtaining help.

FIGURE 2.1   The Classic Windows Desktop.

WEB INTEGRATION AND THE ACTIVE DESKTOP

One of the most important features of Windows 98 is the Active Desktop, shown in Figure 2.2. The Active Desktop combines the aspects of the Classic Desktop with some of the features of a Web browser.

Channel bar: provides access
to Internet channels

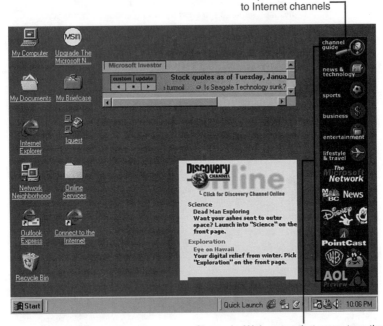

Channels: Web pages that are automatically
updated on your system as they change

FIGURE 2.2   The Active Desktop can display Web pages in
addition to the Classic Desktop content.

 Web Browser   A Web browser is a program used to
view Web pages on the World Wide Web. Web pages
often contain graphics, text, animations, and other special
elements, and a Web browser is designed to display
these elements properly. Popular Web browsers include
Microsoft's Internet Explorer and Netscape Communication Corporation's Netscape Communicator.

With the Active Desktop, you can have up-to-date Web content at
your fingertips without the hassle of constantly logging onto the
Internet, starting your Web browser, and selecting a Web page to
view. For example, you might want to display current stock
prices, news, weather, or even updates from your company's local

intranet. In Lesson 3 you'll learn how to display Web content on your Active Desktop.

The Active Desktop can also affect how you browse your files and folders. Unlike the Classic Desktop, in which you usually double-click to open a folder or file, with the Active Desktop, you single-click instead. This feature (called Web Style) enables you to open files and folders more quickly. (You'll learn more about this feature in Lesson 10, "Drive, Folder, and File Management Options.")

Windows 98 even comes with special toolbars that you can use to access Web pages you visit frequently. You'll learn how to use the Windows 98 toolbars later in this lesson.

TURNING ON THE ACTIVE DESKTOP

By default, the Classic Desktop is displayed when you first start Windows. You can switch to the Active Desktop at any time. Remember—the two Desktops offer many of the same features, except that the Active Desktop lets you display and access Web content more easily. Also, with the Active Desktop, the Web style option that allows you to single-click to open files and folders, is turned on initially (although you can turn it off if you like). You can also use the Web Style option with the Classic Desktop.

To turn on the Active Desktop, follow these steps:

1. Right-click an open area of the Desktop. A shortcut menu appears.

2. Click Active Desktop. A cascading menu appears with more options.

3. From the cascading menu, select View As Web Page. The Active Desktop is displayed.

That's it! When the Active Desktop option is initially turned on, you won't see much of a change. The Channel bar appears, and with it, you can subscribe to the channels you want to display. You'll learn how to do that in Lesson 3, "Subscribing to Channels and Working Offline." Also, the Web Style option is turned on, meaning that you now point to objects to select them and click objects to open or activate them. If you don't want to use the

Web Style option with Active Desktop, right-click the Desktop, select Active Desktop, and then select Customize my Desktop. Click Folder Options, click Yes, select Classic style, and click OK.

Connecting to the Internet   Since the Active Desktop's main duty is to display Web content, it requires that you be connected to the Internet to be effective—if not all the time, *then at least when you initially turn the option on.* If you haven't yet established an Internet connection for your PC, the Connection Wizard appears. See Appendix B, "Configuring for the Internet or an Online Service," for help in using the Wizard and making your first connection.

Switching Back to the Classic Desktop

After using the Active Desktop for a while, you might want to switch back to the Classic Desktop. Switching back and forth between the two Desktops doesn't remove any customization or channel selections you have made.

Remove Those Icons   You don't have to have the icons on the Desktop appear when you're using the Active Desktop. To remove them, right-click the Desktop and select Properties. Click the Effects tab, and select the option Hide icons when the desktop is viewed as a Web page. Then click OK. When you switch to the Classic Desktop, the icons will reappear.

To switch back to the Classic Desktop, follow these steps:

1. Right-click an open area of the Desktop. A shortcut menu appears.

2. Select Active Desktop. A cascading menu appears.

3. Select View As Web Page. This removes the check mark in front of the command, turning the option off. The Classic Desktop appears.

If the Web Style option is turned on in Active Desktop, it remains on when you switch to Classic Desktop. To turn it off, right-click the Desktop, select Active Desktop, and select Customize my Desktop. Click Folder Options, click Yes, select Classic style, and click OK. If you switch back to Active Desktop, the Web Style option won't be turned on, because you turned it off while using Classic Desktop. To turn it back on, right-click the desktop and select Active Desktop | Customize my Desktop | Folder Options | Yes | Web style

USING THE TASKBAR

At the bottom of the Desktop is the taskbar. In addition to the Start button, the taskbar can contain many elements, as shown in Figure 2.3.

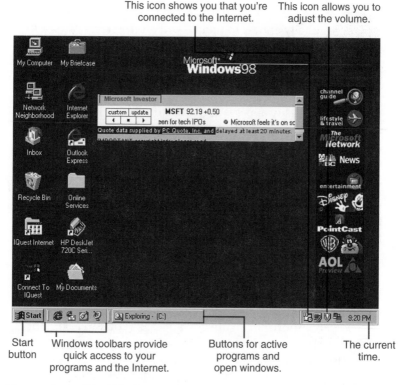

FIGURE 2.3   The Windows taskbar.

- **Start button** With the Start button, you can select commands to open programs, customize Windows, locate files, and search the Internet.

- **Active programs and open windows** Your currently running programs and any open windows such as folder windows appear as buttons on the taskbar. To switch to an open program or window, simply click its button.

- **Toolbars** Windows contains several toolbars that provide quick access to popular programs and functions, such as Web addressing. These toolbars include Address, Links, Desktop, and Quick Launch. In addition, you can create your own toolbars. See Lesson 5, "Using Toolbars and Menus," for help.

- **Status area** At the right end of the taskbar, icons will occasionally appear to update you on the status of various things such as the current time, your Internet connection status, whether you have new email messages in your inbox, and so on.

The taskbar initially appears at the bottom of the Desktop; however, you can move it to the top, left side, or right side by simply clicking it, holding down the left mouse button, and dragging it where you want it.

You can also hide the taskbar and then cause it to appear only when needed. Hiding the taskbar gives you more room on your Desktop for viewing your programs. To hide the taskbar, follow these steps:

1. Click the Start button. The Start menu appears.

2. Select Settings. A cascading menu appears.

3. Select Taskbar & Start Menu. The Taskbar Properties dialog box, shown in Figure 2.4, appears. (You can also right-click the taskbar and select Properties to display the Taskbar Properties dialog box.)

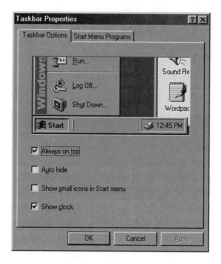

FIGURE 2.4   The Taskbar Properties dialog box.

4. Click the Auto hide option.

5. Click OK. Left-click on the Desktop. The taskbar disappears. To make it reappear, move the mouse pointer toward the taskbar's former location. The taskbar will reappear.

Quick Hide   You can also hide the taskbar by dragging it out of sight. Just move the mouse pointer to the top edge of the taskbar (the pointer changes to a black two-headed arrow) and drag the top of the taskbar down and out of sight. To bring the taskbar back in view, position the pointer along the bottom edge of the screen so that the two-headed arrow activates. Then drag the taskbar back into view.

USING THE WINDOWS 98 TOOLBARS

Windows 98 comes with several toolbars that you can use to access the Internet and your programs more quickly. Some of these toolbars initially appear on the taskbar. You can remove them and place them on the Desktop when needed for more convenient access.

A *toolbar* is a bar of buttons that represent various commands. When you click the appropriate button, the associated command is carried out. Just like the toolbars you often find in Windows programs, a Windows 98 toolbar might contain text boxes in which you can type a command, or list boxes from which you can make a selection.

Here are the Windows 98 toolbars:

- **Address**   When you type an Internet address here, such as the address of a Web page, and press Enter, Internet Explorer will open to display the location you entered.

- **Links**   This toolbar provides access to some popular Internet Explorer links (Web sites).

- **Desktop**   Displays the icons that appear on your Desktop, allowing you to access them when the Desktop is covered with open windows.

- **Quick Launch**   Provides easy access to Internet Explorer, Outlook Express, your Desktop, and the Active Channel Viewer.

- **Custom**   You can create your own toolbars as well.

To display a toolbar, follow these steps:

1. Right-click the taskbar and select Toolbars from the shortcut menu that appears.

2. Click the toolbar you want to display. The toolbar appears on the taskbar.

To use a toolbar, simply click one of its buttons. If the toolbar has a text box (such as the one on the Address toolbar), click inside the text box and type your information (in this case, the address of the Web page you want to display).

To remove a toolbar from the taskbar, right-click the taskbar, se-lect Toolbars, and select the toolbar you want to remove.

You can move or adjust the amount of space the toolbar takes up on the taskbar by dragging its *handle*—the ridge that appears on the toolbar's left edge. Or, if you like, you can drag a toolbar off the taskbar and onto the Desktop. Click anywhere on the toolbar, press and hold down the left mouse button, and then drag the toolbar onto the Desktop, releasing the mouse button when the toolbar is in position. Once the toolbar appears on the Desktop, you can resize it just like any other window. See Lesson 4, "Work-ing with Windows," for help. To close a toolbar that is on the Desktop, click the Close button (× in the upper-right corner of the Window.

CREATING A TOOLBAR

You can create your own toolbar by selecting New Toolbar from the Toolbars menu. Select the folder whose contents you want to display as a toolbar, or type in the address of a Web page, and then click OK. If you select a folder, a toolbar with icons repre-senting the contents of that folder appears. You could then click an icon for a document, for example, to open that document with its associated program. If you enter the full address of a Web page, starting with "http://" that page appears on the toolbar itself. To see the page, drag the toolbar off the taskbar.

Keep in mind that the toolbars you create are only temporary. If you close one, you'll need to create it again to get it back. If, how-ever, you keep the toolbar open, it will remain open and active even if you restart your PC.

In this lesson, you learned the differences between the Classic Desktop and the Active Desktop. In addition, you learned how to switch between the two as needed. You also learned how to use the taskbar and the Windows 98 toolbars. In the next lesson, you'll learn how to display Web content on your Active Desktop.

SUBSCRIBING TO CHANNELS AND WORKING OFFLINE

In this lesson, you'll learn about the Web and how it fits into Windows 98. In addition, you'll learn how to display Web content on your Desktop and how to customize that display to fit your needs.

INTERNET BASICS

The Internet is a vast worldwide network of networks that connects various businesses, government offices, universities, research centers, and so on. Through the Internet, you can access data from these networks, such as scientific research, sales and product information, and travel and weather data.

You connect to the Internet through an Internet service provider (ISP). You can connect to an ISP via a modem (called a *dial-up connection*) or through your company's network (a *direct connection*). If you need help setting up your Internet connection, see Appendix B, "Configuring for the Internet or an Online Service."

The World Wide Web supports the transmission of graphics, sound, animations, and formatted text—unlike other parts of the Internet, which are strictly text-based. Thus, the part of the Internet you'll visit most often will probably be the Web.

To view Web pages (the documents that make up the World Wide Web), you need a Web browser. Windows 98 comes with Internet Explorer, a popular Web browser from Microsoft; however, you might want to use Netscape Communicator from Netscape Communication Corporation instead. Both are compatible with Windows 98. In Lessons 24 and 25, you'll learn how to use Internet Explorer. If you decide to use Netscape Communicator, you'll find that the general Web searching techniques described in Lessons 24 and 25 apply to it as well.

Most Web browsers (including Internet Explorer and Netscape Communicator) have components that handle the non-WWW elements of the Internet, so you won't have to install a bunch of special programs in order to send and receive email or visit newsgroups. For example, you'll learn how to use Outlook Express to send and receive email and to view newsgroups in Lessons 26 and 27.

WHAT IS A SUBSCRIPTION?

As you learned in Lesson 2, "Navigating the Windows 98 Desktop," Windows 98 offers two different Desktop options. The Active Desktop lets you display active (live) Web content on your Desktop, where it is easily accessible. To select the content you want to display, you set up a *subscription*. A subscription allows you to obtain current information from an Internet source. The information is refreshed right on your Desktop at intervals you select.

You can display the contents of various channels or the contents of a conventional Web page on your Desktop. A *channel* is a special Web page that can update itself, changing the Desktop display by constantly adding up-to-date information. The Active Desktop uses *push technology*—the idea being that, through channels, businesses on the Web can automatically push their information to your computer instead of your having to log onto their Web site and *pull* the data down.

 Pay to Play?   Currently, it costs you nothing to subscribe to most channels, although that might change in the near future.

MSNBC is an example of one channel to which you might subscribe. You can select from many different kinds of channels with the Channel bar. A subscription (a live, constantly updated Web page) is typically displayed in a full-screen window, although you can resize the window to display other subscriptions at the same time if you want.

In addition, Microsoft offers many Active Desktop items (such as stock tickers and weather displays) through its Active Desktop Gallery. A Desktop item is displayed in a small window on the Desktop (see Figure 3.1). Note you have to remain connected to the Internet to maintain live channel or Active Desktop item content on your Active Desktop.

You can also display a *static* (conventional) Web page (one that doesn't automatically update) on your Desktop. For example, if you find a Web page you like, you might want to view it on your Desktop. Such a page can automatically be downloaded to your system once a day (or following whatever schedule you prefer). After the page has been updated for the day, its contents on your Active Desktop don't change.

Subscribing to a Channel

When you first display the Active Desktop, it contains no active Web content. To select what you want to display, you subscribe to either a channel or a static Web page. You can add as many Active Desktop items to the Desktop as you want.

Connect First   In order to complete these steps, you must have already established your Internet connection. See Appendix B for help.

To subscribe to a channel, follow these steps:

1. If needed, change to the Active Desktop by right-clicking the Desktop, selecting Active Desktop from the shortcut menu, and selecting View As Web Page.

2. If the Channel bar doesn't appear on your Desktop, display it by selecting Active Desktop | Customizing my Desktop, and then choose Internet Explorer Channel Bar on the Web tab of the Display Properties dialog box.

3. Click a channel (such as the Disney channel) or a category (such as entertainment) on the Channel bar, as shown in Figure 3.1. You can also select channels through the Start menu by choosing Favorites and then Channels.

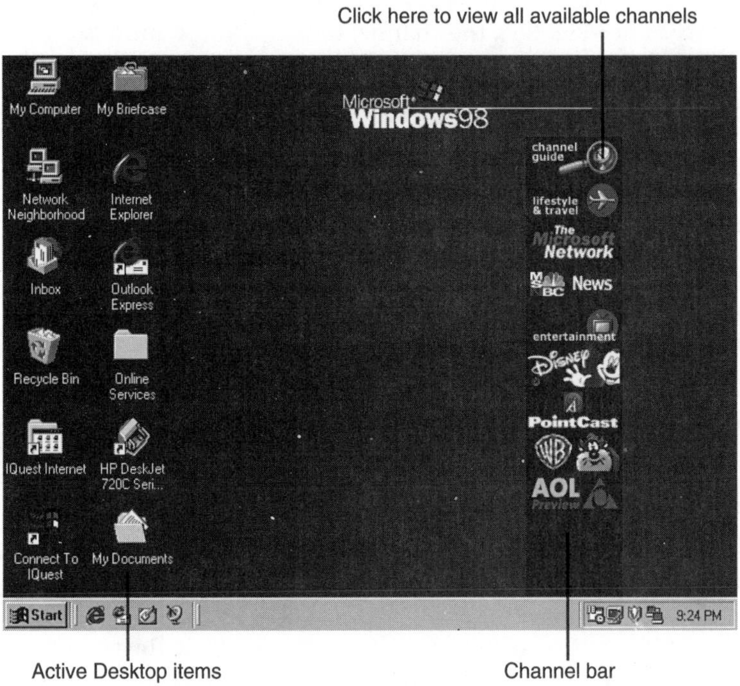

Click here to view all available channels

Active Desktop items   Channel bar

FIGURE 3.1   To subscribe to a channel, select it from the Internet Explorer Channel bar.

Channel Selector   To view all the channels available to you, select Channel Guide from the Channel bar. Internet Explorer downloads the current list of channel categories. Click a category such as Sports, and a list of channels appears. Additional channels can be viewed by selecting the ranges of numbers in the Findings column. Select the channel you want to add by clicking its logo.

4. If you're not currently connected to the Internet, you'll see a dialog box prompting you to connect. Click the Connect button. A Dial-Up Connection dialog box appears. Click Connect to connect to the Internet.

5. If you selected a category (such as News & Technology), you need to click the channel to which you want to subscribe. After you select a channel, it appears in the Internet Explorer window. Each channel is set up a bit differently, so follow the onscreen instructions to subscribe to the channel you select. Typically, you need to click a button called Add Active Channel or Subscribe.

6. When you add a channel, the Modify Channel Usage dialog box, shown in Figure 3.2, appears. Select the option you desire:

> No, just keep it in my Channel Bar   This option adds the channel to the Channel bar as a button. You can then use this button to quickly display the channel's contents, since the channel *will not* be updated on your system automatically.

> Yes, but only tell me when updates occur   This option lets you control when a channel is updated on your system. When a change occurs, you'll be notified. You can then choose to update the channel. You might want to choose this option if you connect to the Internet via modem.

> Yes, notify me of updates and download the channel for offline viewing   This option automatically updates your channel and then tells you that the channel has been updated. This option is good if you have a permanent (network) Internet connection.

> Customize   Use this option to control exactly when and how the channel is updated. See the next section for details.

7. If the channel you select has a screen saver, you'll be asked if you'd like to replace your current screen saver with it. Click Yes or No, as you prefer.

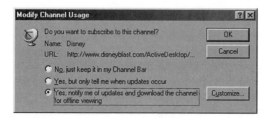

Figure 3.2   Select how or if you want the channel to be updated.

Initially, channels appear full-screen on the Desktop. To reduce them to the size of a window, click the Full Screen button on the toolbar at the top of the screen. You can then resize the window as needed in order to view more than one channel at once.

Some channels offer an option for adding a Desktop item as well. Follow these steps:

1. Follow the preceding steps to display a channel you like. When you see the option to add a Desktop item, click Add to Active Desktop.

2. You'll see a message asking if this is okay. Click Yes.

3. You'll see a verification dialog box confirming your selection. Click Yes. To change the frequency at which the Desktop item is updated, click Customize Subscription and then follow the steps in the next section.

You can move Active Desktop items. Move the mouse pointer to the top of the item's window, and a title bar appears. Click this title bar, click and hold the mouse button, and drag the window wherever you like.

You might also prefer to remove the Desktop icons in order to make more room for Web content. To do so, right-click the Desktop and select Properties. Click the Effects tab and select the option Hide icons when the desktop is viewed as a Web page. Click OK.

Customizing a Subscription

You can easily customize when a channel is updated to your system through the Customize option that appears in the Modify Channel Usage dialog box. Follow these steps:

1. In the first screen of the Subscription Wizard, you can choose to Download only the channel home page or Download all content specified by the channel (which might be several pages). Make your selection and click Next >.

2. When a channel page changes, Internet Explorer notifies you by adding a red gleam to the channel page's icon. If you'd also like to be notified by email, select Yes. Otherwise, select No. Click Next >.

3. Select how often you would like this channel updated. If you're connected to the Internet though a network, you might want to use the Scheduled option. If you choose this option, select the schedule you want to use from the drop-down list, or create one of your own by clicking New. If you select the Scheduled option and you use a modem to connect to the Internet, be sure to select the option Dial as needed if connected through a modem as well.

   However, if you connect through a modem, you might prefer to select Manually. If you select this option, the page will be updated when you choose Update All Subscriptions from the Favorites menu of the Scheduled Tasks accessory (select Programs | Accessories | System Tools | Scheduled Tasks to reach the menu) or right-click on the Desktop and select Active Desktop | Update Now. (See the section "Working Offline and Updating Subscriptions" for more information on how to manually update a channel.) If you select New to create your own schedule for updating the subscription, continue to step 4. Otherwise, click Finish.

4. Select Daily, Weekly, or Monthly, and then select the Days on which you want the update to occur (either every

weekday or at intervals you select—for example, every 3 days).

5. Select the Time at which you want the update to occur (either the exact time or at intervals you select).

6. If you want to allow Windows 98 to vary the actual update time by a few minutes (in order to avoid all the other users who have selected the same time), choose Varies exact time of next update to improve performance.

7. When you're through making your selections, click OK. You're returned to the Subscription Wizard. Click Finish. You will then be returned to the Modify Channel Usage dialog box. Click OK.

You can change the update schedule of an existing subscription by right-clicking its logo on the Channel bar and selecting Properties. Click the Schedule tab, and then make the appropriate selections on the tab to change the schedule.

Subscribing to a Web Site or an Active Desktop Gallery Item

In addition to subscribing to a channel, you can select items from Microsoft's Active Desktop Gallery for use on your Desktop. You can also display the contents of a static Web page on your Desktop. Simply follow these steps:

1. If needed, change to the Active Desktop by right-clicking the Desktop, selecting from the shortcut menu, and then selecting.

2. Right-click the Desktop and select from the shortcut menu that appears. Then select.

3. Click the Web tab in the Display Properties dialog box, as shown in Figure 3.3.

4. Click.

5. You'll be asked if you want to visit Microsoft's Active Desktop Gallery. If you do, click Yes. If not, click No and skip to step 12.

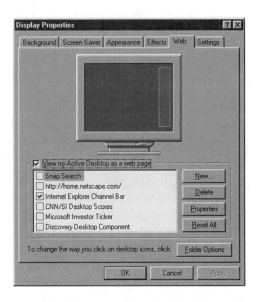

FIGURE 3.3   Adding a Web page or Gallery item to the Desktop.

6. If you're not currently connected to the Internet, you'll see a Dial-Up Connection dialog box prompting you to connect. Click the Connect button to connect to the Internet.

7. The Gallery appears in an Internet Explorer window. Click a category such as News.

8. Click an item to view its description. For example, click Microsoft Investor Ticker.

9. A page describing the item you selected appears. Click Add to Active Desktop.

10. A confirmation box appears; click Yes to continue.

11. The Add item to Active Desktop (TM) dialog box appears; click OK to add the item to your Desktop. If you want to change the time at which the item is updated, click Customize Subscription and follow the steps in the preceding section to customize the item.

12. If you answered No in step 5, the New Active Desktop Item dialog box, shown in Figure 3.4, appears.

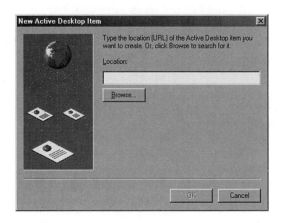

FIGURE 3.4   Adding a static Web page to the Desktop.

13. Type the address of the Web page you want to add to the Desktop in the Location text box, and click OK.

14. The Add item to Active Desktop (TM) dialog box appears; click OK. If you want to customize the way in which the page is updated, click Customize Subscription and follow the steps in the preceding section. If the site requires a password, you will need to choose Customize Subscription and enter the password.

15. You're returned to the Display Properties dialog box. Click OK.

Using a Web Page as Your Desktop

In Lesson 8, "Customizing the Appearance of Windows 98," you'll learn how to select a color or a graphic image for use as your Desktop background. You can also use a Web page as your Desktop if you like. However, unlike channels, the Web page won't be automatically updated on your Desktop when the live Web page changes on the Web.

First, download a copy of a Web page to your hard disk (using the File | Save As command in your Web browser), and then select the page from those listed on the Screen Saver tab of the Display Properties dialog box. See Lesson 8 for more details.

Working Offline and Updating Subscriptions

If you have a dial-up (modem) connection to the Internet, you probably won't be connected to the Internet at all times. Whenever you're not connected, you're considered to be working *offline*.

When you select a channel or perform any other Web-related task when you're not currently connected to the Internet, you'll see a dialog box prompting you to connect. To continue working offline, click the Work Offline button.

When you work offline, your subscriptions won't be updated. You can update them manually by connecting to the Internet, right-clicking the Desktop, selecting Active Desktop from the shortcut menu, and selecting Update Now from the cascading menu (or you can select it from the Start menu—Start | Settings | Active Desktop | Update Now.

You can also manage your subscriptions with the Scheduled Tasks accessory, which you'll learn more about in Lesson 23, "Disk Management." For now, follow these steps:

1. Click the Start button, select Programs, select Accessories, select System Tools, and select Scheduled Tasks. The Scheduled Tasks accessory appears.

2. Open the Favorites menu and select Manage Subscriptions. A Subscriptions window similar to the one shown in Figure 3.5 appears.

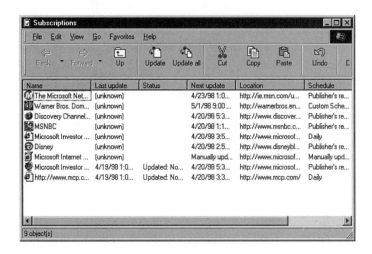

FIGURE 3.5   You can update all or just one of your subscriptions.

3. To update a single subscription, click it and then click the
   Update button on the toolbar at the top of the window.
   To update all your subscriptions, click the Update all button. (You can also select Update All Subscriptions from
   the Favorites menu.)

 Update Automatically   If you connect to the Internet
through your modem, you can tell Windows to log onto
the Internet when needed and to update your subscriptions automatically. See the section "Customizing a Subscription" for help.

You can also update a subscription by right-clicking its logo on
the Channel bar and selecting Update Now.

CANCELING SUBSCRIPTIONS

After setting up a subscription, you might want to unsubscribe to it (cancel it). (To change the update schedule for an existing subscription, see the section "Customizing a Subscription.") Follow these steps:

1. Click the Start button, select Programs, select Accessories, select System Tools, and select Scheduled Tasks. The Scheduled Tasks accessory appears.

2. Open the Favorites menu and select Manage Subscriptions. The Subscriptions window, shown in Figure 3.5, appears.

3. Right-click on the subscription you want to change, and select Properties.

4. Click the Subscription tab. Then click the Unsubscribe button. A Confirm Item Delete dialog box will open. Click Yes to remove this subscription permanently.

Rather than unsubscribing to it, you can temporarily hide an Active Desktop item by following these steps:

1. Right-click the Desktop, select Active Desktop, and select Customize my Desktop. The Display Properties dialog box appears.

2. Click the Web tab, and then click the check box in front of the item you want to hide to remove the check mark. The item disappears from the sample area at the top of the dialog box.

3. Click OK.

In this lesson, you learned about the Internet as it relates to the Active Desktop. You learned how to subscribe to channels, Gallery items, and static Web pages. You also learned how to adjust schedules for updating Web content is updated and how to remove Web items from your Active Desktop. In the next lesson, you'll learn how to open, close, resize, and move windows.

WORKING WITH WINDOWS

4

In this lesson, you'll learn how to open, close, resize, move, arrange, and scroll through the contents of windows.

WHAT IS A WINDOW?

A *window* is a container for data (such as files, folders, programs, icons, and so on). Depending on your preference, a window can occupy a particular region of the screen or the entire screen. Figure 4.1 shows the parts of a typical window.

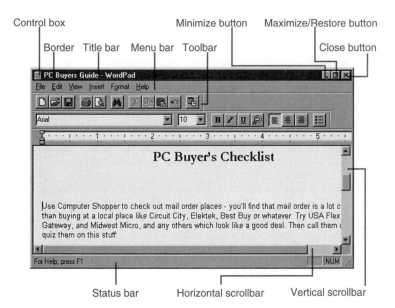

FIGURE 4.1 Parts of a typical window.

Here is a brief description of each of the elements:

Control box   Provides a menu with commands for controlling the window's size, closing the window, and moving the window. Generally the control box contains the identifying icon for the program that uses this window. For example, in Figure 4.1, the icon for WordPad serves as the control box. On an Active Desktop Item (a window that contains Web content), the control box looks like a down arrow.

Border   The frame that surrounds the window. You can resize a window by stretching its border.

Title bar   Displays the title of the window, which includes the name of the program (if applicable) and the name of its active file.

Minimize button   Click this button to remove the window from the screen temporarily.

Maximize/Restore button   Click the Maximize button, and the window fills the screen; click the Restore button to return the window to its former size.

Close button   Click this button to close (exit) a window and its associated program.

Vertical scrollbar   Use this scrollbar to view data hidden above or below the displayed data.

Horizontal scrollbar   Use this scrollbar to view data hidden to the left or right of the displayed data.

Menu bar   Contains the main categories of commands you give to an application. When you click one of these main categories, its list of associated commands drops down, and you can select a command or pull up a submenu from that list. You'll learn how to use menus in Lesson 5, "Using Toolbars and Menus."

Toolbar   Most applications use toolbars; they contain buttons you can click to perform common commands such as printing, opening, and saving a document.

Status bar   Most applications include a status bar at the bottom of the window. It alerts you to changes in the program and provides other useful information.

OPENING A WINDOW

Generally, windows open themselves when you launch an application or when you open a document within that application.

When you launch an application from the Start menu, from a Windows Explorer listing (discussed in Lesson 10, "Drive, Folder, and File Management Options,"), or by double-clicking its icon on the Desktop, the application responds by opening its own main window. For an application such as WordPad, which comes with Windows 98, the window that pops up will be empty, ready for you to enter data into it and save that data as a document file. But for more sophisticated applications such as Word 97, that empty document window might be contained within the application's main window.

 Single-Click Option   Double-clicking typically means "Open up!," but if you're using the Web Style option, you can set up Windows to open a window with a *single-click* on a filename, folder, or icon. See Lesson 10, "Drive, Folder, and File Management Options," for help.

SWITCHING BETWEEN WINDOWS

Before you work with the contents of a window, that window must be active. For example, to use a particular program, you must activate the window in which it's contained. Regardless of how many windows you have open at the time, you can only have one *active* window. The active window appears with a brighter title bar than the other open windows (typically blue under the standard Windows 98 default desktop settings).

To activate a window (in other words, to switch from one window to another), you can perform any of the following tasks:

- Click any part of the open window
- Press Alt+Tab to scroll through the list of open windows
- Click the window's button on the taskbar

SIZING A WINDOW WITH MAXIMIZE, MINIMIZE, AND RESTORE

A window can be maximized (made to fill the screen) or minimized (removed from the screen temporarily). To maximize a window, click its Maximize button (see Figure 4.1). When the window is already maximized, this button changes to the Restore button. Click this button to restore the window to its former size, revealing part of the Desktop. You might want a window to be maximized when you're concentrating on its application specifically. On the other hand, when you're working with more than one application at the same time, you might want to see all of their respective windows simultaneously. In that case, you will want to leave them at their restored size. To quickly maximize a window, double-click on its title bar. Then, to restore a window to its original size, double-click the title bar again.

The Minimize button removes the window from the Desktop without terminating (closing) its program. To restore the window so that you can start using the program again, click that program's button, which appears on the taskbar.

 Don't Minimize the Usefulness of This Tip   To quickly minimize a window, double-click its button on the taskbar.

MINIMIZING ALL WINDOWS

To minimize all your windows at once so that only the Desktop is visible, do the following:

1. Right-click an *empty* portion of the taskbar (where there are no minimized application buttons).

2. From the pop-up menu that appears, select Minimize All Windows.

To restore your windows, right-click the taskbar again and select Undo Minimize All.

If you're currently displaying the Quick Launch toolbar on your taskbar, you can also use it to minimize all your open windows. Simply click the Show Desktop button.

 My Web Windows Are Still There!   Using the Minimize All Windows command doesn't affect the Active Desktop Items (the windows that contain Web content) you might be displaying on your Active Desktop. To remove them temporarily, switch back to the Classic Desktop. Right-click the Desktop, select Active Desktop, and then select View As Web Page to turn the option off. To return to the Active Desktop, repeat these steps.

Sizing a Window's Borders

While a window is not maximized, you can change its size by dragging its border. When you stretch or shrink a window, you can move one side or corner at a time. Here's how:

1. Move the mouse pointer to one edge or corner of the window. The pointer changes to a black two-headed arrow.

 No Arrow?   If you don't see a two-headed arrow when you move the mouse pointer to a window's border, the window size probably can't be changed.

2. While the pointer is a two-headed arrow, click and hold down the left mouse button.

3. Drag the mouse pointer in the direction you want to stretch or shrink the window. As you're dragging, the window size will change.

4. When the window is the size you want, release the mouse button.

 Can't Resize a Window? Many applications' windows have minimum applicable sizes. So if the window doesn't budge, but the pointer continues to move, the window is as small as it can be.

USING SCROLLBARS

Scrollbars are used to display contents that extend beyond the window's current viewing area. Figure 4.2 shows a window with both horizontal and vertical scrollbars.

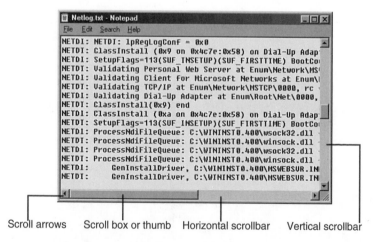

FIGURE 4.2 A window with both scrollbars active.

Here's how you use scrollbars:

- To move by a small amount, click the arrow at either end of the scrollbar that points in the direction you want to move.

- To move by a larger amount, click the open space on either side of a horizontal scroll box, or above or below a vertical scroll box.

- To move quickly through a document, drag the scroll box along the scrollbar to whatever position you choose. Many Windows programs move the contents of the window as you move the scroll box; others wait until you release the button to execute the move. Some programs provide a screen tip that displays the relative page number in the document as you drag the scroll box. The screen tip lets you quickly scroll to the exact page you want.

MOVING A WINDOW

The title bar displays the name of the program being used by the window, as well as the name of the current active document. The supplemental function of the title bar is as a handle of sorts. To move a window onscreen, click and drag the window's title bar. When you move a window in Windows 98, the contents of the window follows your movements. If you want to switch back to the Windows 95 method (which displays only the window outline as you move), right-click the desktop, select Properties, click the Effects tab, and turn off the Show window contents while dragging option.

 Can't Move a Maximized Window?   You can't move a window that's been maximized. There's no place for it to go.

You can also move Active Desktop Items, such as the one shown in Figure 4.3. Here's how:

1. Move the mouse pointer toward the top of the Active Desktop Item. A title bar should appear.

2. Click this title bar and drag the window wherever you like.

3. Release the mouse button. The window is repositioned.

Title bar ⎯⎯⎯⎯  ⎯⎯Close button

Figure 4.3   Moving an Active Desktop Item is similar to moving any other window.

Arranging Windows on the Desktop

When you have more than one window open simultaneously—say, three or four—and all of them are pertinent to the job you're working on, stretching and shrinking all of them so that they fit precisely might be inconvenient. Thankfully, Windows 98 has a few ways for you to automatically arrange several windows *without* the drag-and-drop maneuver.

Cascading Windows

All the windows in a *cascaded* set overlap one another so that the upper and left borders are always visible—not unlike the way you would fan out a hand of gin rummy. Figure 4.4 shows a set of four cascaded windows.

FIGURE 4.4 A set of cascaded windows.

Here is how you can make Windows automatically cascade all
open windows on the Desktop:

1. Right-click an *empty* portion of the taskbar.

2. From the shortcut menu that appears, select Cascade
   WindowsThe Cascade Windows command doesn't affect
   Active Desktop Items.

TILING WINDOWS

By comparison, each window in a *tiled* set (whether the tiling is
horizontal or vertical) doesn't overlap in any way. Figure 4.5
shows the same four windows as Figure 4.4, this time tiled horizontally.

All tiled windows are of equal size. If you have a large number of
windows open, tiling can result in rather small windows.

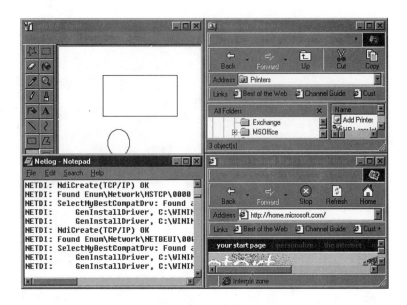

Figure 4.5   A set of horizontally tiled windows.

To tile your open windows, right-click an empty portion of the taskbar and select either Tile Windows Horizontally or Tile Windows Vertically. The Tile commands don't affect Active Desktop Items.

Closing a Window

When you're finished with a window, you should close it. This frees up system resources for other activity. Closing a program's window is the same thing as exiting the program.

Some windows will immediately close themselves when you click the Close button; other windows—especially programs with open files—might ask if you want to save information before closing the window. This gives you an opportunity to save your open files before exiting the program. You can also close a window from the taskbar; just right-click the program's button, and select Close.

You can also close Active Desktop Items by clicking their close buttons (see Figure 4.3). Closing an Active Desktop Item temporarily removes it from the Active Desktop. To get the window back, right-click the Desktop and select Active Desktop from the shortcut menu. Then select Customize my Desktop. Click the Web tab, and then click in the box in front of the Active Desktop Item you want to redisplay. A check mark appears in front of the window you select. Click OK.

In this lesson, you learned the various parts of a window. You also learned how to move, resize, minimize, maximize, and close a window. In addition, you learned how to operate scrollbars and how to arrange windows on the Windows 98 Desktop. In the next lesson, you'll learn how to use toolbars and select menu commands.

5 USING TOOLBARS AND MENUS

In this lesson, you'll learn how to use the toolbars that come with many Windows programs. You'll also learn how to select commands from menus.

USING TOOLBARS

Not every Windows program uses a toolbar, but many do. A *toolbar* is a collection of buttons that represent commands. When you click a button, the associated command is executed.

 What About Windows Toolbars? In this lesson, you'll learn how to use the toolbars included with many Windows programs, such as Windows Explorer and My Computer. If you want to learn how to use the Windows 98 toolbars, see Lesson 2, "Navigating the Windows 98 Desktop."

Because toolbars offer access to the most common commands, many programs have toolbars that contain the same buttons. Figure 5.1 shows Windows Explorer and its toolbars.

The Cut button is a common type of toolbar button. You select the files you want to move and then click the Cut button. Notice the order of events here: You always select the object of your command *first,* and *then* click the button—not the other way around.

The Back button in Windows Explorer is another type of button. The down-arrow to the right of the icon indicates the presence of a drop-down list. If you click the Back button, the Windows Explorer window moves back to the previous directory (or Web page). But if you click the down-arrow portion of the Back button, a menu drops down, showing the most recent directories (or Web pages) in Windows Explorer's history buffer. You then choose the directory you want to move back to by clicking it in the list.

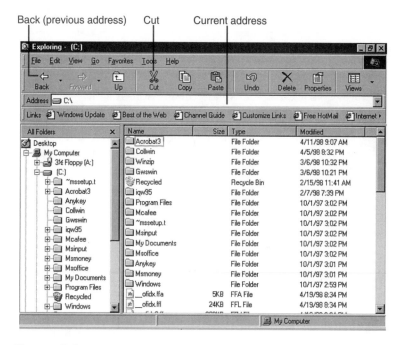

FIGURE 5.1   Windows Explorer and its toolbars.

The Address box is an example of a third type of toolbar button: a drop-down list box. The Address box drops down when you click the down-arrow button, revealing a menu—in this case, the hierarchy of the current directory. You choose the directory you want Windows Explorer to move to by clicking it.

Most toolbars you will use are comprised of some combination of these three types of controls.

Common Toolbars

Many Windows programs such as Windows Explorer and My Computer use the same standard toolbars: Standard Buttons, Address boxes, and Links. The purpose of the buttons on each of these toolbars is explained in Tables 5.1, 5.2, and 5.3. (Note the Links toolbar buttons link to web pages, and the contents of the toolbar may vary).

Table 5.1   The Standard Buttons Toolbar

Button	Name	Purpose
	Back	Displays the previous folder.
	Forward	Redisplays the folder viewed immediately before the Back button was pressed.
	Up	Moves up in the folder hierarchy.
	Cut	Moves the selected file or folder to the Clipboard. (See Plain English below).
	Copy	Copies the selected file or folder.
	Paste	Pastes the contents of the Clipboard into the current folder. (See Plain English below).
	Undo	Undoes the last action.
	Delete	Removes the selected file or folder.
	Properties	Displays the properties of the selected file or folder.
	Views	Lets you select the way in which files and folders are displayed.

Clipboard   A tool provided by Windows that holds any cut or copied text temporarily in memory so you can paste it to another location, document, or application.

TABLE 5.2   THE ADDRESS TOOLBAR

NAME	PURPOSE
Address	Lets you enter or select the address of the folder you want to view.

TABLE 5.3   THE LINKS TOOLBAR

NAME	PURPOSE
Best of the Web	Displays links to some of the best pages on the Web in categories such as Business, Computers & Internet, and Entertainment.
Channel Guide	Displays a listing of channels to which you can subscribe.
Customize Links/ To Customize	Display a page that show you how to customize the Links bar.
Free HotMail	Displays the hotmail from Microsoft (a free Web-based email service) Web page.
Internet Start	Displays the Microsoft Internet Start Web page.
Microsoft	Displays the Microsoft Web page.
Internet Explorer News	Displays the Internet Explorer Web page.
Windows Update	Displays the Windows Update Web page.

MOVING TOOLBARS

Not all toolbars in Windows can be moved from place to place. A clear signal that a toolbar *can* be moved is the presence of a handle—single ridge near the left edge (or the top edge in the case of a vertical toolbar). You might want to move a toolbar to a different location for short-term convenience. For example, you might want to move a toolbar into the work area to make it easier to work with a particular bit of text or a graphic image.

Here are some general methods for moving toolbars:

- To move a toolbar into the work area, click an empty space on the toolbar and drag the toolbar wherever you like. Typically, the toolbar will then take on a more rectangular shape, which you can adjust as you might adjust the size of a window.

- To move a toolbar so that it appears *underneath* another toolbar, drag it by the handle on top of the toolbar under which you want it to appear, and release the mouse button.

- To adjust the boundaries between two toolbars that are horizontally adjacent to each other (for example, the Address and the Links toolbars in Windows Explorer), position the pointer between the two toolbars so that it changes to a black two-headed arrow. Then drag the border in either direction.

- To swap positions between two toolbars sharing the same line (such as the Address and Standard toolbars in Windows Explorer), click the handle of one of the toolbars. Then drag the handle past the handle of the other toolbar.

USING MENUS

The menu bar is a Windows program's chief device for presenting you with its available commands. Menu bars are typically placed just under the title bar in a window (see Figure 5.2), although some programs let you move the menu bar to a different position onscreen (Windows Explorer is one such example).

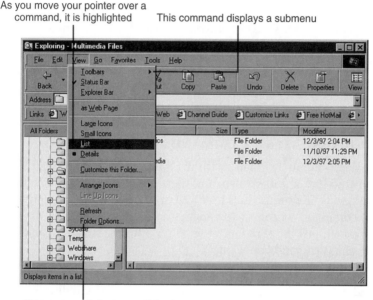

As you move your pointer over a command, it is highlighted   This command displays a submenu

This command displays a dialog box

FIGURE 5.2   A typical menu.

When you open one of the menus on a menu bar, a list of related commandsdrops down. You can select any of the commands on the menu. Here is a brief listing of what typically happens when you choose a command:

- Most commands are executed by the program immediately after you select them. Cut and Paste are classic examples. Once you select them, the program carries them out without delay and without asking you anything else.

- If a command has a right-pointing arrow, a submenu (a cascading menu) with additional choices will appear. For example, in Windows Explorer, if you open the File menu and select New, a submenu appears. The submenu in this case lists various objects such as folder, shortcut, bitmap image, and so on that answer the question "New *what?*"

- If a command is followed by an ellipsis (...), the command requires more information from you before it can be executed. Thus, when you select such a command, a dialog box appears with several options from which you can choose. For example, the File | Open... command in Microsoft Word displays a dialog box from which you can select the file you want to open.

Choosing Menu Commands

To select a menu command with the mouse, you click one of the menus so that it drops down, and then you click one of the menu commands. If a submenu is involved, it will pop up to the right of that command (or to its left if there's no room to the right). At that point, just move the mouse pointer onto the submenu and click the command you want.

If you don't see the command you need, or if you change your mind, you can click anywhere *outside* the menu area to dismiss the menu altogether. Or you can move the pointer to another menu category, without clicking, to have its menu drop down instead.

To use the keyboard to select a menu command, press and hold down the Alt key as you press the underlined letter of the menu command. For example, to open the File menu, press Alt+F. Once the menu is opened, press the underlined letter of the command you want. For example, to select the Open command from the File menu, press the letter O. You can also use the up- and down-arrow keys on the keyboard to move the highlight line to the command you want and then press Enter to select the command.

Using Shortcut Keys

Many commands provide another method for you to select them with the keyboard—without having to open the menu first. For

example, the common commands Cut, Copy, and Paste have
shortcut key combinations that you can press to select them:
Ctrl+X for Cut, Ctrl+C for Copy, and Ctrl+V for Paste. For example, to issue the Copy command, press and hold down the Ctrl
key as you press the letter C. Shortcut keys are listed next to their
corresponding command on menus. For a complete listing of the
shortcut keys associated with the program you're using, consult
that program's Help system, under the term "shortcut keys" or
"keyboard shortcuts."

USING SHORTCUT MENUS

As an alternative to using the menu bar or toolbars, you can issue
commands to many Windows programs using a right-click
method, which brings up a *shortcut menu* or *context menu*. With
this method, you point to the item onscreen that is the object of
your command—for instance, a highlighted sentence or a row of
cells in a worksheet. You then right-click. If the program supports
shortcut menus, one will pop up onscreen, as shown in Figure
5.3. From there, you can click a menu command to issue that
command to the program or click outside the menu area to dismiss the menu.

FIGURE 5.3   You can access common commands with a shortcut
menu.

The reason that a shortcut menu is also called a context menu is
because the commands that are displayed are related to whatever
the mouse was pointing to when you right-clicked.

Default Command   On the shortcut menu shown in Figure 5.3, the command Explore is bold. This means that Explore is the default command—the command that will be executed if you double-click this object (in this case, the Windows folder).

Shortcut menus are available outside applications as well. For example, if you right-click the Desktop, a shortcut menu appears from which you can select commands that arrange your icons, switch you between the Active and Classic Desktops, and change the Desktop's properties.

In this lesson, you learned how commands are issued to Windows programs. You studied the operation and arrangement of toolbars onscreen. You then examined the role played by the menu bar in all Windows applications, and you were introduced to the shortcut menu, which provides a convenient alternative to the menu bar. In the next lesson, you'll learn how to select options from dialog boxes.

Using Dialog Boxes

In this lesson, you'll learn how to select options using all types of dialog box elements, such as text boxes, list boxes, option buttons, and checkboxes.

When a Dialog Box Appears

A dialog box typically appears after you select a menu command marked with an ellipsis (...). The ellipsis tells you that the command you selected requires more information from you before it can be executed by the program. The dialog box provides the means by which you can tell the program which options to use with the command.

Selecting Dialog Box Options

Windows uses a handful of standardized elements that work the same way for any dialog box you encounter. To move through the objects in the dialog box, press the Tab key. To back up to the previous element, press Shift+Tab. Here's a listing of the elements and how to use them:

- **Text box** A box into which you type text, such as the name of a file, the key number on the back of the Windows 98 CD, or a password to access the Windows 98 Desktop. To replace existing text, drag over it to highlight the text, and then type what you want to replace it. Figure 6.1 shows a dialog box that contains a text box control.

- **List box** A rectangle that lists several choices, the way a menu does. If there are more entries in the list than can be shown at once, a scrollbar appears along the right and/or bottom edges. For a list box that supports multiple choices (such as a file list), to select more than one item at a time, hold down the Ctrl key and click each item. You can also hold down the Shift key and click the first and last item in a range to select all the items in that range. A list box is shown in Figure 6.1.

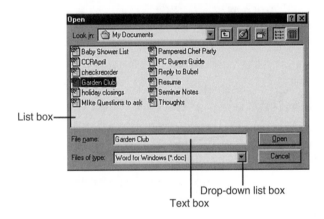

FIGURE 6.1   A text box and a list box.

- **Drop-down list box**   A variation of a standard list box; the list is revealed when you click the down-arrow. To select something from the list, click it. You can't change or add to the items in the list. Figure 6.1 shows a drop-down list box.

- **Combo box**   A hybrid of the text box and list box. The top line of a combo box works like a regular text box, featuring a blinking cursor. You may type a choice into this box or choose one from the list below the text line. A combo box supports only one choice at a time.

- **Check box**   Click the box next to the item you select to place a check mark in the box. Check boxes may be grouped together. If they are, you can choose more than one option. Figure 6.2 shows a group of check boxes.

You can only select   Tabs create several "pages"   You can select more
one option button.   within a dialog box.   than one check box.

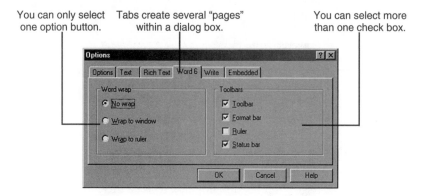

FIGURE 6.2   A tabbed dialog box featuring check boxes and option buttons.

- **Option button**   This type of button is also known as a *radio button*. You click the circle or label beside an item to select it. Unlike the check box, you can choose only one option in the set. Figure 6.2 shows a dialog box with a set of option buttons.

- **Command button**   The most common button in a dialog box. The OK and Cancel buttons are command buttons. After making selections in a dialog box, click OK to issue the command with the options you selected, or click Cancel to *not* issue the command. Most dialog boxes have a *default* command button, which is generally the OK button. Press Enter at any time while the dialog box is active to activate the default command button; press Esc to dismiss the dialog box without issuing the command.

Keyboard Shortcut   If a dialog box contains controls whose labels have certain letters underlined—holding down the Alt key while pressing the underlined letter will immediately move the focus to the labeled element and select it (or deselect it, if the item was previously in selected mode). For example, in Figure 6.2, holding down the Alt key and pressing "N" highlights the "No wrap" item (by placing a box around it) and activates the "No wrap" feature. To immediately reverse the selection, press the spacebar or the underlined letter.

TABBED DIALOG BOXES

Many dialog boxes have *tabs* that compartmentalize information into multiple pages. A tabbed dialog box looks a little like a file drawer, where you would thumb through the tabs sticking up in order to find the folder you want. A tabbed dialog box is shown in Figure 6.2.

To change pages in a dialog box, click one of the tabs. Using the keyboard, press Ctrl+Tab to move to the next tabbed page in the sequence, or press Shift+Ctrl+Tab to move to the previous one.

In this lesson, you learned how to make selections in a dialog box using the most common elements: text boxes, list boxes, drop-down list boxes, check boxes, option buttons, and command buttons. In the next lesson, you'll learn how to access help.

USING WINDOWS 98 HELP

In this lesson, you'll learn about the Windows 98 Help system, including the Contents, Index, Search, and What's This features.

GETTING HELP IN WINDOWS 98

Help is always close at hand in Windows. When you press F1 while viewing files from My Computer or Windows Explorer, or when another Windows program is active, the Help system is activated. The Help window that appears usually coincides with whatever action you were performing. You can also activate Help by clicking the Start button and selecting the Help command.

The Help window appears with two panes. The left one is used to navigate Help, and the right one displays information on a help topic. Also included are five buttons:

- Hide/Show   Hides (or redisplays) the left Help pane (the Table of Contents).

- Back   Returns you to a previously viewed Help page.

- Forward   After you've used Back, this button redisplays a previously viewed Help page.

- Options   Displays a list of Help options.

- Web Help   Provides a link to Microsoft help on the World Wide Web.

Quick Dialog Help   In addition to pressing F1 to activate Help, most dialog boxes feature a Help button that you can click to get help in choosing the options in that dialog box.

In this lesson, you'll learn how to navigate the Windows 98 Help system to locate the information you're looking for.

Help consists of three parts:

- Contents   A table of contents you can browse through.

- Index   Similar to the index in the back of a book.

- Search   Lets you search the Help system for a particular word or phrase.

You'll learn how to use all three of these features in this lesson.

Do You Use the Web Style Desktop?   Help is written for the Classic Style Desktop, in which you double-click a filename to open it. If you use the Web Style Desktop, note that when Help tells you to double-click, you'll need to single-click.

Using the Contents Feature

Using the Contents feature is similar to using the table of contents in a book. Here you'll find the major categories of Help. If you select a topic, it expands to display subtopics from which you can choose, as shown in Figure 7.1. The book icons represent topics and subtopics; document icons represent actual Help pages. Selecting a document displays information on that topic in the right pane.

Follow these steps to use the Contents feature:

1. If needed, press F1 or click the Start button and select Help to display the Help dialog box.

2. Click a topic that has a book icon, and it will expand to reveal subtopics.

3. If needed, click a subtopic to expand it.

4. Click a topic that has a document icon to display its contents in the right pane of the Help window (see Figure 7.1).

Major topics   The topic you select is displayed here.

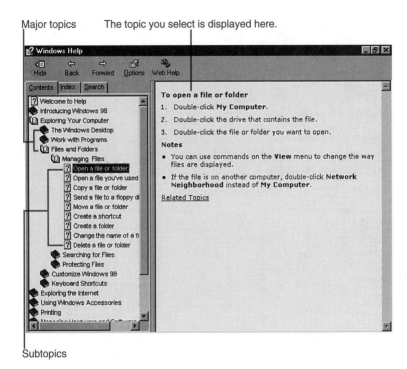

Subtopics

FIGURE 7.1   When you select a topic, it expands.

5. Depending on the topic, you may be presented with the following options in the right pane of the Help window:

   Click here   Click this link to launch related applications and wizards.

   Related Topics   If you click this link, a small window appears from which you can select a related topic.

6. To close Help, click the Close buttonin the upper right corner of the Windows Help window.

USING THE INDEX FEATURE

Help's Index feature is similar to an index you might find at the back of a book. To use it, you type in the word you're looking for, and it appears in a list, as shown in Figure 7.2. Select a topic from this list, and it's displayed in the right pane.

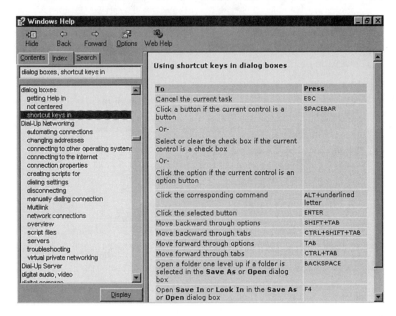

FIGURE 7.2   Use the Index to locate a specific word or phrase.

Follow these steps to use the Index feature:

1. Type a word or phrase in the text box. As you type, Help searches the Index for a match, so you might not actually have to type the entire word you're looking for.

2. Double-click the topic in the list that you would like to display. The topic appears in the right pane. (A dialog box of selections may appear; if so, select the subtopic you want and click Display.)

USING THE SEARCH FEATURE

Index lets you search for a match to your word or phrase within a *topic heading*. Search lets you search for a match *within the contents* of the topic itself; this expands the possibility of locating a match.

After using the Contents and Index features to locate what you want, try using Search. Follow these steps:

1. Type the word or phrase you want to search for in the text box, and then press Enter or click List Topics.

2. A list of topics is displayed. When you double-click a topic, it appears in the right pane, as shown in Figure 7.3.

Type your word or phrase here   Select a topic from this list

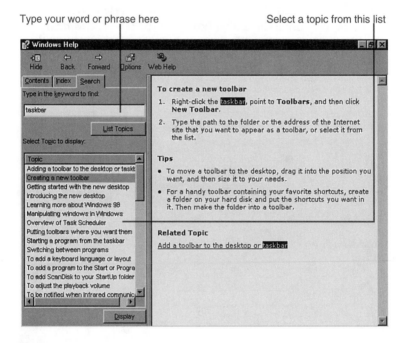

FIGURE 7.3   Search allows you to search the text within Help topics.

USING THE WHAT'S THIS? FEATURE

Many Windows dialog boxes include a What's This? button. After you click it, you can click any option within that dialog box and view a description of it. This feature lets you quickly decide which options within a dialog box you want to use.

When a dialog box includes a What's This? button (shown in Figure 7.4), follow these steps to use the What's This? feature:

1. Click the What's This? button. The mouse pointer changes to show a question mark along side it.

2. Click any option within the dialog box. A description of that option appears.

3. After reading the description, click anywhere in the dialog box to remove the dialog box from the screen and turn off the What's This? feature.

When you click an option with the What's This? pointer, a description appears.   What's This? button

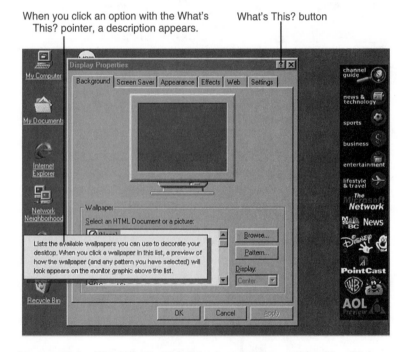

FIGURE 7.4 The What's This? feature helps you identify which dialog box options you might want to use.

 Quick Description To display a description of a dialog box more quickly, just right-click it and select What's This? from the shortcut menu that appears.

Using Web Help

For users who have access to the Internet, Windows 98 includes a Web Update feature that can be used for Windows 98 support.

The Windows Update site, like many Web sites, may change its content frequently, so the specific steps to follow and the selections available at the time you access the site may vary from those described in this lesson.

To locate answers to common Windows questions, follow these general steps:

1. Connect to the Internet if you are not already connected.

2. Click the Start button and select Windows Update. Internet Explorer starts and connects to Microsoft's Update site.

3. Click Support. You might be asked if you would like to register. Click Yes and follow the instructions in the Registration Wizard that appears.

4. You may see a security warning. Click Yes to continue.

5. Select a topic that interests you from the My Search is about list.

6. Type the keywords for the item you want help with in the I want to search for text box.

7. Click Find.

You might also want to click the How To or the Glossary links displayed on the Web page. They provide additional help: How To describes how to search for information, and Glossary defines Windows' terms.

Obtaining Help in Updating Your System

If you have access to the Internet, Windows Update can help you keep your system current. For example, if you experience a problem with your computer, you can use Windows Update to update

your Windows software, download the latest drivers for your
hardware, and obtain service updates and bug fixes. Updating
your system will often solve your problem.

 Driver A driver is a special program that lets a particular
hardware device, such as a CD-ROM or a sound card,
communicate with your computer.

To update your Windows system, follow these general steps (note,
as mentioned in the previous section, that the specific steps to
follow and selections available may vary, depending on the current Web page content):

1. Connect to the Internet if you are not already connected.

2. Click the Start button and select Windows Update.
   Internet Explorer opens and connects to Microsoft's Windows Update site.

3. To update your system, click Product UpdatesUpdate
   Wizard. You're taken to theProduct Updates Web page.

4. You might be asked if you would like to register. Click Yes
   and follow the instructions in the Registration Wizard
   that appears.

5. You may see a security warning. Click Yes to continue.

6. Select components you would like to install and press
   "Start Download." The components will be downloaded
   and installed on your computer.

7. To check for new system files and device drivers available
   for your PC, follow the instructions on the Web page
   regarding Device Drivers and System Files. Typically you
   will be guided through the steps by an Update Wizard

In this lesson, you learned how to use the Windows Help system,
including its Contents, Index, Search, and What's This? features.
You also learned how to use the Windows Update feature to update your system and get product assistance. In the next lesson,
you'll learn how to customize the appearance of Windows 98 to
suit your needs.

CUSTOMIZING THE APPEARANCE OF WINDOWS 98

In this lesson, you'll learn various ways in which you can customize Windows 98 to fit your needs.

ARRANGING ICONS ON THE DESKTOP

The icons on your Windows Desktop provide quick access to the programs you use most often. However, if the icons are placed on the Desktop haphazardly, it becomes difficult for you to find the icon you want when you need it.

You can, of course, drag each icon into place manually. But to quickly arrange the icons on the Desktop in neat rows, follow these steps:

1. Right-click the Desktop and select Arrange Icons from the shortcut menu.

2. Select a command from the cascading menu that appears:

    by Name   Arranges the icons alphabetically.

    by Type   Arranges the icons by their type (their filename extension).

    by Size   Arranges the icons by the size of their files.

    by Date   Arranges icons by their file date (the date they were created or changed).

    AutoArrange   Arranges icons automatically. If you add an icon to the Desktop, it's automatically arranged with the other icons in neat rows.

You can also arrange your icons in neat rows by right-clicking the Desktop and selecting Line Up Icons.

Icons and the Active Desktop   You can completely remove icons from the Active Desktop and avoid the problem of having to arrange them all the time. Right-click the Desktop and select Properties. Click the Effects tab and select the Hide icons when the desktop is viewed as a Web page option.

CHANGING THE BACKGROUND OF THE DESKTOP

Initially, the Desktop is a solid teal color. Instead of a plain color, you can use a graphic as "wallpaper" to cover the background. You can choose a Windows graphic or use one of your own. (If you want to change the color of your Desktop background, and you don't want to use a graphic or a pattern, see the section "Changing the Appearance (Colors) of Windows.")

Bitmap Image   A bitmap image is a graphic format in which the image is stored as a series of pixels or dots. The pattern of dots forms a bitmap.

You can also choose a pattern to use as your Windows background (but you can't use both a wallpaper graphic and a pattern). You can even edit these patterns to customize the look of your Desktop if you like.

Follow these steps to select a graphic for your Windows Desktop:

   1. Right-click the Desktop and select Properties. The Display Properties dialog box, shown in Figure 8.1, appears.

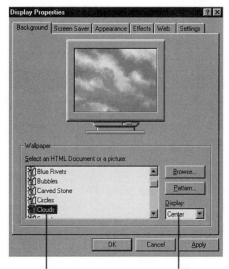

Select your graphic   Select how to display the graphic

FIGURE 8.1   Wallpaper your Desktop with a nice graphic.

2. Select a graphic from the Wallpaper list. A preview of your selection appears at the top of the dialog box.

 I Prefer My Own, Please   If you'd like to use your own graphic as a background (perhaps something you've downloaded from the Internet), click Browse and select the graphic from the list. You can use .BMP, .GIF, and even .JPG images.

3. Select Tile, Center, or Stretch from the Display drop-down list. Tile arranges the graphic across the Desktop in neat rows; Center places the graphic image in the center of the Desktop. Stretch does just what the name implies: it stretches the graphic image so that it fills the entire desktop.

4. To test the graphic on your Desktop, click Apply. If you don't like the result, select another graphic and click Apply again.

5. When you're satisfied with your selection, click OK.

 System Too Slow?   You might notice a small degradation in performance when you use a graphic or a pattern as a background, since they both use more of your system resources.

Follow these steps to select a pattern for your Windows Desktop:

1. Right-click the Desktop and select Properties. The Display Properties dialog box appears (see Figure 8.1).

2. If you were previously using a graphic for your background, select None from the Wallpaper list.

3. Click Pattern. The Pattern dialog box, shown in Figure 8.2, appears.

FIGURE 8.2   You can use a pattern as a background for your Desktop.

4. Select a pattern from the list. To edit the pattern, click Edit Pattern. Otherwise, skip to step 6.

5. Click within the Pattern box to change the pattern one pixel at a time. You can give your variation a new name by typing that name in the Name text box. When you're through, click Change to save your changes. Then click Done.

6. In the Pattern dialog box, click OK.

7. To test the pattern on your Desktop, click Apply. If you don't like the result, follow steps 3 through 6 to select another pattern, and click Apply again.

8. When you're satisfied with your selection, click OK.

ADDING A SCREEN SAVER

A screen saver prevents a display from becoming static for a long period of time, which might cause a permanent imprint (or burn-in) of the screen on your monitor.

 Screen Saver Not Needed? Newer monitors have a feature that allows them to automatically turn themselves off after so many minutes of inactivity. If you have such a monitor, a screen saver is not needed—although you can still use one.

You can purchase any number of more entertaining screen savers, or you can use the screen savers that come with Windows 98.

To turn on the Windows 98 screen saver, follow these steps:

1. Right-click the Desktop and select Properties. The Display Properties dialog box appears (see Figure 8.1).

2. Click the Screen Saver tab. The Screen Saver page appears, as shown in Figure 8.3.

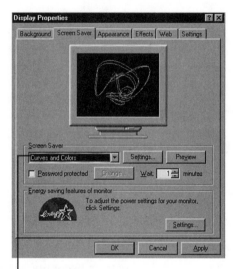

Select the screen saver you
want to use from this list

FIGURE 8.3   Windows 98 offers several screen savers from which
you can choose.

3. Select the screen saver you want to use from the Screen
   Saver list. A preview appears at the top of the dialog box.

4. In the Wait text box, enter the number of minutes of
   inactivity you want Windows to wait before initiating the
   screen saver.

5. Click Settings to access the options available for the particular
   screen saver you selected. Make your changes and click OK.

6. If you want to protect your PC from unauthorized use
   when you're away from your desk, select the Password
   protected option, click the Change button, enter a password, and click OK. You will then have to enter this password to gain access to your system whenever the screen
   saver is initialized.

7. Click OK when you're through.

Power Management Options   To save energy when your PC is not in use, you can have your monitor (and the hard disks) put themselves into "suspended animation." To access the Power Management options, click the Settings button in the Screen Saver dialog box.

CHANGING THE APPEARANCE (COLORS) OF WINDOWS

Windows uses a particular color scheme by default. This color scheme determines the color of the title bars of active and inactive windows, the color of the Desktop, the style of the window text, the size and spacing of icons, and so on. You can select a different color scheme entirely, or change only the colors of individual elements. Here's what to do:

1. Right-click the Desktop and select Properties. The Display Properties dialog box appears (see Figure 8.1).

2. Click the Appearance tab. The Appearance page, shown in Figure 8.4, appears.

3. Select a color scheme from the Scheme drop-down list. A preview of the scheme appears at the top of the dialog box.

4. If you want, you can change the color and style of individual Windows elements. Select the element you want to change from the Item drop-down list and then select the color or style you desire.

5. When you're through making selections, click OK.

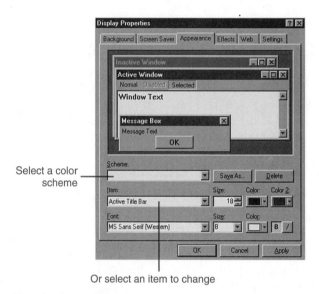

Select a color scheme →

Or select an item to change

FIGURE 8.4   Windows lets you customize its appearance.

CHANGING HOW ICONS ARE DISPLAYED

When you first install Windows 98, your Desktop has several icons for basic Windows items, such as My Computer and the Recycle Bin. You can exchange these icons for something else if you think they aren't meaningful.

In addition to changing the icons on the Desktop, you can also elect to show larger icons, and to display those icons using the entire spectrum of colors available to your monitor.

 More Space Required?   If you want to adjust the amount of space between icons, do so with the Appearance tab, as explained in the preceding section.

To change the icon options, follow these steps:

1. Right-click the Desktop and select Properties. The Display
   Properties dialog box appears (see Figure 8.1).

2. Click the Effects tab. The Effects page appears, as shown
   in Figure 8.5.

Click here to restore an icon

FIGURE 8.5   Visual options are available on the Effects tab.

3. To change one of the Desktop icons, click it and then
   click Change Icon. Windows opens a file of default icons
   from which you can choose. Select one and click OK. (If
   you have another icon file you want to use instead, click
   Browse to select the file first.)

4. If you want to use large icons, or you want to display your
   icons using all possible colors, select those options.

5. When you're done, click OK.

Hide Those Icons   If you use the Active Desktop, to hide the icons from view, right-click on the Desktop and select Properties from the shortcut menu. Click the Effects tab and select the option Hide icons when the desktop is viewed as a Web page.

CHANGING THE SCREEN RESOLUTION

Resolution settings are identified by the number of pixels (or dots) they use horizontally and vertically. For example, 640-by-480 resolution uses 640 pixels horizontally and 480 pixels vertically. 640-by-480 resolution is typically the lowest you can use. In addition to the number of pixels, you can control the range of colors your monitor uses. The more colors, the better the display of certain graphics, but this will take up more video memory.

When you use a higher resolution, the images might become clearer, but your icons and text will become smaller. This is because, with more pixels on-screen, the relative size of each pixel is smaller. To compensate for this, you can choose the Large Fonts option—just click the Advanced button in the Settings dialog box. (To increase the size of the icons, use the Effects tab, as explained in the preceding section.)

To change your screen resolution, follow these steps:

1. Right-click the Desktop and select Properties. The Display Properties dialog box appears (see Figure 8.1).

2. Click the Settings tab, shown in Figure 8.6. If you're using more than one monitor, select the monitor whose settings you wish to change.

3. To change to a higher resolution, drag the Desktop area slider toward More. To switch to a lower resolution, drag the slider toward Less.

4. Select the number of colors you want to use from the Colors drop-down list box.

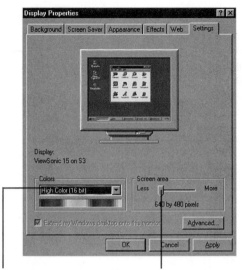

Select a color palette   Move slider to change screen resolution

FIGURE 8.6 Changing the resolution affects how items are displayed onscreen.

5. If you're using two monitors and you would like to use them in synch (to display a single image of your Desktop), select the second monitor in step 2 and then select the Extend my Windows desktop onto this monitor option.

6. Click OK when you're done.

Change Often? If you change your screen resolution often, you can place an icon on the taskbar for fast access to the Display Properties dialog box. To place an icon on the taskbar, click the Advanced Properties button and select the Show settings icon on taskbar option.

In this lesson, you learned how to customize Windows by arranging icons, changing the background, selecting a screen saver, changing colors, changing how icons are displayed, and selecting a different screen resolution. In the next lesson, you'll learn additional ways to customize Windows.

CUSTOMIZING OTHER ATTRIBUTES OF WINDOWS 98

9

In this lesson, you'll learn various ways in which you can customize the taskbar, as well as sounds and mouse settings.

CHANGING THE TASKBAR

The taskbar is your Windows lifeline, providing access to your programs, Windows settings, often-used documents, and Help. This section will show you how to customize the taskbar to suit your work style.

SETTING TASKBAR OPTIONS

Windows provides several options with which you can customize the taskbar and its Start menu. Follow these steps:

1. Click the Start button and select Settings. Then select Taskbar & Start Menu from the cascading menu that appears. The Taskbar Properties dialog box appears, as shown in Figure 9.1.

2. Select the options you want:

    Always on top   This option causes the taskbar to appear on top of any window, so you can always see it.

    Auto hide   This option causes the taskbar to disappear. To make it reappear, move the mouse pointer toward its former location.

    Show small icons in Start menu   The main Start menu uses large icons, which can make it quite wide.

(Submenus off the Start menu use small icons.) To make the main Start menu less wide, choose this option.

Show clock   This option causes the current time to display on the taskbar.

3. When you're done, click OK.

The display
changes to
reflect the
options you
select

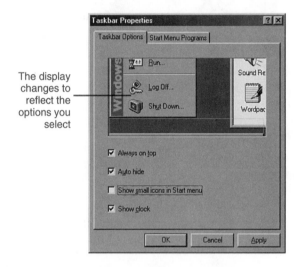

Figure 9.1   It's easy to customize the taskbar to suit your needs.

Reorganizing the Start Menu

When you install a new program, that program automatically adds a command to start itself to your Start menu.

You might prefer to reorganize the commands for your programs into groups that you find more logical. You may also want to add your DOS programs (because they don't automatically add their commands to your Start menu), or you might prefer quick access to some of your folders. In any case, it's easy to customize the Start menu, as these steps show:

1. Click the Start button and select Settings. Then select Taskbar & Start Menu from the cascading menu that appears. The Taskbar Properties dialog box appears (see Figure 9.1).

2. Click the Start Menu Programs tab. To add a new command to the menu, click Add.

3. Type the path to the command you want to add, or click Browse and select it from the file list. Click Next>.

4. Select the menu (folder) under which you want your command to appear. You can create a new menu by clicking New Folder and typing a name. Click Next>.

5. Type a name for the command as you want it to appear on the menu. Click Finish.

To remove a menu command, click Remove in step 2. Then select the command you want to get rid of and click Remove.

To clear the Documents menu (which normally shows the last 15 files you've worked on), click the Clear button on the Start Menu Programs page in the Taskbar Properties dialog box.

Fast Reorg   You can reorganize the commands that are already on the Start menu by opening the Start menu, clicking on an item, and simply dragging it wherever you would like it to be.

CREATING YOUR OWN TOOLBARS

As you learned in Lesson 2, "Navigating the Windows 98 Desktop," Windows 98 comes with several toolbars that provide fast access to the Internet and to some commonly used programs such as Internet Explorer. These toolbars initially appear on the taskbar, but they can be dragged onto the Desktop if needed.

You can create your own toolbars to add to this collection. The toolbar will display the contents of whichever folder you select.

 Custom Shortcuts If you want to create a toolbar that has icons for your favorite programs, create a folder and then add program shortcuts to it. To create a program shortcut, open Explorer and drag the program's file into the folder you created.

To create a toolbar, follow these steps:

1. Right-click an open area of the taskbar and select Toolbars from the shortcut menu that appears. Select New Toolbar from the cascading menu.

2. Select a folder, or type an Internet address (if you want to create a toolbar that you can later drag onto the Desktop to display that Web page in a window).

3. Click OK. The toolbar appears on the taskbar.

To remove the toolbar from the taskbar, right-click it and select Close from the shortcut menu. This deletes the toolbar permanently; you will need to redo the preceding steps to re-create it. You can, however, keep the toolbar on the taskbar as long as you like—even restarting your PC won't remove it. You can also drag the toolbar off the taskbar onto the Desktop just like the other toolbars; doing so *will not* delete your new toolbar.

Changing the Sounds for System Events

You can replace the sounds that are played for system events (such as displaying a program error and exiting Windows) with ones you create or download from the Internet. You can also re-place the default Windows sounds with another sound scheme, such as Jungle. Here's how:

1. Click the Start button and select Settings. Then select Control Panel from the cascading menu that appears.

2. Click or double-click the Sounds icon. The Sounds Properties dialog box, shown in Figure 9.2, appears.

Select an event

Select a sound for the event

Click to test sound

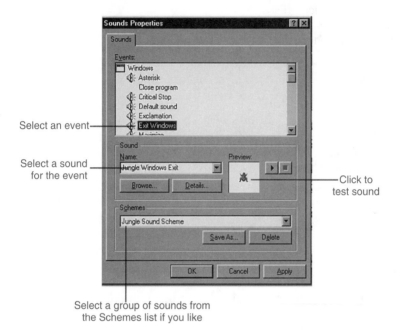

Select a group of sounds from the Schemes list if you like

FIGURE 9.2   Change how Windows sounds with the Sounds Properties dialog box.

3. From the Events list, select the event whose sound you want to change.

Sound Coordination   If you would like to coordinate your sounds around a theme, Windows 98 offers several sound Schemes from which you can choose.

4. Select a sound file from the Name list, or click Browse and select your own sound file. To listen to the sound, click the right-arrow button in the Preview area.

5. Click OK.

ALTERING THE DATE AND TIME

The time that appears on the taskbar is based on the clock setting for your computer. If it's off, you need to adjust the computer clock. To do so, follow these steps:

1. Click the Start button, select Settings, and then select Control Panel. In the Control Panel window, click or double-click the Date/Time icon. The Date/Time Properties dialog box appears.

 Fast Times   To display the Date/Time Properties dialog box quickly, double-click the time icon on the right end of the taskbar.

2. To change the system date, click on a new date.

3. To change the system time, use the spinner that appears under the clock.

4. Click OK.

MODIFYING MOUSE SETTINGS

If you find that you're having trouble getting the mouse to click or double-click properly, you might try adjusting its sensitivity. You can also increase the size of the mouse pointer if you find that you're having trouble locating the mouse onscreen. To change these and other mouse settings, follow these steps:

1. Click the Start button, select Settings, and then select Control Panel. In the Control Panel window, click or double-click the Mouse icon. The Mouse Properties dialog box appears.

2. If you're left-handed, you can switch the functions of your mouse buttons by selecting the Left-handed option from the Button configuration panel. To adjust the speed at which your mouse recognizes a double click, drag the slider in the Double-click speed panel. For example, if you find it hard to click twice fast, move the slider toward Slow. To test the setting, double-click the box in the Test area. If a jack-in-the-box appears when you double-click, the setting is fine. Make adjustments as needed.

3. Click the Pointers tab. Here you can select a different set of mouse pointers from the Scheme list box. For example, you might want to select Animated hourglasses or 3D Pointers if you want to jazz things up. Or you might want to select Windows Standard (large) or Windows Standard (extra large) if you're having trouble seeing the mouse pointer.

4. Click the Motion tab. To adjust the speed at which the mouse moves across the screen, drag the Pointer speed slider. If you use a laptop and you find that the mouse pointer is getting lost, turn on the Show pointer trails option and use the slider to adjust its speed.

5. Click OK when you're done selecting options.

In this lesson, you learned how you can customize Windows to suit your tastes. In the next lesson, you'll learn how to manage your files, folders, and drives using My Computer and Explorer.

10 DRIVE, FOLDER, AND FILE MANAGEMENT OPTIONS

In this lesson, you'll learn various ways to manage your files, folders, and disk drives using both My Computer and Windows Explorer.

UNDERSTANDING DRIVES, FOLDERS, AND FILES

Most computers come with at least two disk drives: the hard disk drive and the floppy disk drive. The hard disk drive provides large-capacity storage for your programs and the data files you create. Windows itself is also stored on the hard disk drive. The floppy disk drive lets you transfer small amounts of data from one computer to another easily.

The drives are assigned letters so that the computer can tell them apart. Typically, the hard disk is drive C: and the floppy disk drive is A:. Your PC might have more than one hard disk, or the hard disk might be divided into separate partitions. If so, the additional drives are labeled D:, E:, and so on. If your PC has more than one disk drive, it is labeled B:. If your PC has a CD-ROM drive, it's assigned the first available drive letter, such as D: or E:.

Typically, a new folder is created for each program you install on the hard disk. You can create additional folders to organize your data into manageable units, just as you might organize your work papers into various folders within your file cabinet.

Files are placed into each folder, just as you might place individual pieces of paper into a file folder. There are two basic file types: *program files* (files that are used to run an application) and *data files* (files that contain data created by an application). You can mix both types within a folder if you want.

Filenames under Windows 98 can contain up to 255 characters, with a three-character extension. Although there are some characters you can't use (/ \ ; * ? > < |), this still gives you a fair amount of freedom in assigning your files names that will help you later identify their purpose, such as "Sales for 4th Quarter 1997." Note that filenames can include both letters and numbers *and also spaces*.

 Extension   A file's extension identifies its purpose. For example, a filename that ends with the extension .TXT contains only text. A filename that ends in .EXE is a program file, and a filename that ends in .BMP is a bitmap graphic file. There are many other file types, but you don't need to learn them, because Windows specifies the type of file in the Type column in both My Computer and Explorer.

 Naming Your Files   If you still use any old DOS programs, you'll have to restrict the names for the files you create with those programs to eight characters or less (no spaces). These older programs don't recognize the longer filenames used by Windows 98. You should also restrict the names you give to the folders you use with those programs to eight characters or less.

Using My Computer

Windows 98 offers two programs with which you can view your files, folders, and drives: My Computer and Windows Explorer. Both are remarkably similar, as you'll soon see. My Computer is shown in Figure 10.1.

Standard Buttons toolbar
Menu bar   File list   Column headers

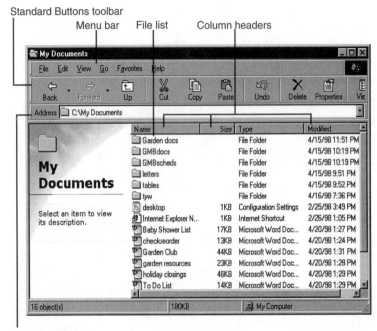

Address toolbar

Figure 10.1   You can view your files, folders, and drives with My Computer.

As you'll learn in upcoming lessons, you use both My Computer and Windows Explorer in the same way:

- To start My Computer, double-click its icon on the Desktop.

- To display the contents of a drive or folder, double-click it.

- To move up the folder hierarchy to a previous folder, click the Up button.

- You can also move from folder to folder or to a different drive by selecting it from the Address drop-down list box.

- To return to a recently displayed folder, open the File menu and select the folder from the list near the bottom of the menu.

- To refresh the display (for example, if you switch disks in a drive and you want to display the contents of the new disk), press F5 or open the View menu and select Refresh.

My Computer does not include a folder hierarchy list (called the All Folders list) in a separate panel on the left as Explorer does. This is the main difference between the two programs. The presence of this list might make it easier for you to quickly jump from folder to folder as you browse (in which case you might prefer to use Explorer), or it might confuse or annoy you (in which case you might prefer to use My Computer).

Also, unlike Explorer, My Computer opens a new window with each folder or drive you explore. You can change this feature by switching to Web Style, as explained later in this lesson.

USING WINDOWS EXPLORER

Windows Explorer is not much different from My Computer, as you can see from Figure 10.2.

As just mentioned, Explorer contains a folder hierarchy (the All Folders list) that you can use to jump from one drive or folder to another. There is another difference between My Computer and Explorer: Explorer lets you use the Tools|Find command (Find is also available on the Start menu) to search your computer or the network for a particular file or folder. (My Computer makes the Find command available only in its main window.) You'll learn how to search for files and folders in Lesson 13, "Creating, Deleting, Renaming, and Finding Files and Folders."

Otherwise, you use Explorer in the same basic manner in which you use My Computer:

- To start Explorer, open the Start menu, select Programs, and then select Windows Explorer.

- Select a folder or file to view from the All Folders list by clicking it.

Address toolbar

Menu bar

All Folders list

Column headers

Standard Buttons toolbar

File list

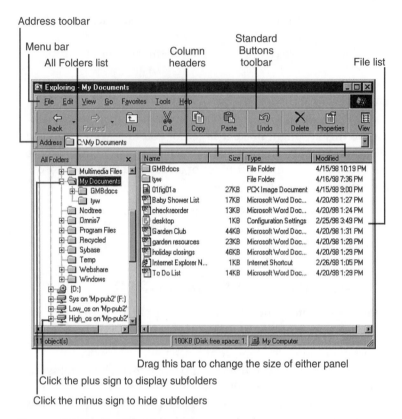

Drag this bar to change the size of either panel

Click the plus sign to display subfolders

Click the minus sign to hide subfolders

FIGURE 10.2 Explorer is another program you can use to view files, folders, and drives.

- If a folder in the All Folders list is preceded by a plus sign, it contains subfolders. To display them, click the plus sign. To hide them again, click the minus sign that appears.

- In addition to using the Up button, you can move from folder to folder by clicking a folder you want to view in the All Folders list.

- You can change the size of either panel by dragging the bar that divides them.

Faster Exploration If you have a Windows keyboard with a key that shows the Windows logo, then you can use a shortcut to launch the Windows Explorer. Press and hold down the Windows key (much like the Shift or Ctrl keys) and then press the E key and release both keys.

UNDERSTANDING WEB STYLE VERSUS CLASSIC STYLE

If you use the Active Desktop, you might be interested in using the Web Style option within My Computer and Explorer. With Web Style, the purpose of clicking and double-clicking is changed. Instead of clicking to select a file, you simply point to it. And instead of double-clicking to open a file, you click it. This change affects not just Explorer, but My Computer and the Desktop as well.

In addition, if you change to Web Style and then use My Computer, each folder you open is displayed in the same window instead of separate windows. If you want to use Web Style's single-click method for selecting and opening folders and files, but want to retain the use of multiple windows in My Computer, then use the Custom option, as explained in the tip later in this lesson.

To change to Web Style:

1. Open the View menu and select Folder Options.

2. On the General tab, select the Web style option.

Separate from Web Style, but often associated with it, is Web view. In Web view, the contents your folders are displayed as Web pages, with icons representing subfolders and files, as shown in Figure 10.3. To display a folder in Web view, click the Views button and select as Web page.

Point to a file to see
its description   Description

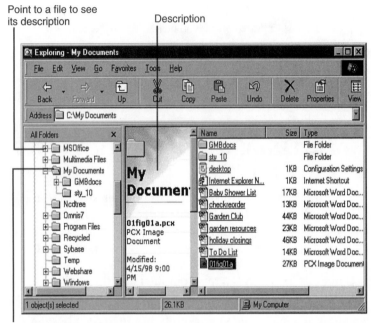

To open a folder, click it

FIGURE 10.3   In Web Style, icons are used to represent files and
folders.

Here are some tips on using Web Style:

- To open a subfolder, you click it, just as you might click a
  link within a Web page.

- To select a file, point to it. A description of the file will
  appear.

- You can browse the Web using Explorer or My Computer.
  Simply type the address of the page you want to view in
  the Address list box.

If you don't want to use Web Style, you can select Classic Style,
which is shown in Figures 10.1 and 10.2.

When you use the Active Desktop, Classic Style is turned on by default. To switch to Web Style, follow these steps:

1. Open the View menu and select Folder Options.

2. On the General tab, select the Classic style option.

3. Click OK.

 I Want It My Way!   If you select the Custom option on the General tab, you can choose the options you want to use with the style you selected, such as single- or double-clicking, and the opening of a new window when you view a folder.

In this lesson, you were introduced to both My Computer and Explorer. You also learned the differences between Web Style and Classic Style. In the next lesson, you'll learn how to use Explorer to view your files and folders and how to customize its display.

LESSON 11

VIEWING DRIVES, FOLDERS, AND FILES

In this lesson, you'll learn various ways in which you can view and sort the files in My Computer and Explorer.

CHANGING THE DISPLAY IN MY COMPUTER AND WINDOWS EXPLORER

As you learned in the preceding lesson, My Computer and Windows Explorer are remarkably similar. All the tasks you will learn in this and subsequent lessons can be performed in either program (unless noted). For simplicity, I will show only Explorer in the figures.

The main difference between the My Computer and Explorer displays is the presence of the All Folders list in Explorer (see Figure 11.1). You can easily remove this list, to provide more room for the file listing, by opening the View menu and selecting Explorer Bar and then selecting None. You can also simply click the Close button (the ×) at the top of the All Folders list.

If you want to display the All Folders list but you would like it to take up less room, you can resize the All Folders panel by dragging the bar that separates it from the file list.

 Not in My Computer!   You can't display the All Folders panel in My Computer. It is strictly an Explorer option.

All Folders list

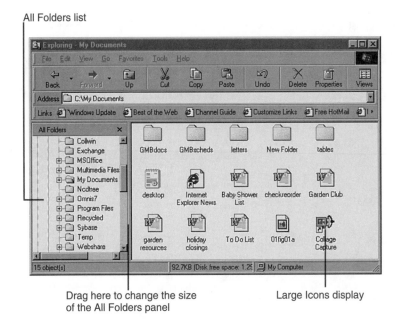

Drag here to change the size   Large Icons display
of the All Folders panel

FIGURE 11.1   The All Folders list provides quick access to your folders.

CHANGING THE FILE LIST DISPLAY

In Figure 11.1, files are displayed using large icons. This is just one of many ways in which you can list your files. To change the File List display, open the View menu and select the view option you want: Large Icons, Small Icons, List, or Details (which provides the file's name, size, type, and date of last modification, as shown in Figure 11.2). The current option appears with a dot beside it on the View menu.

History list   Small icons display

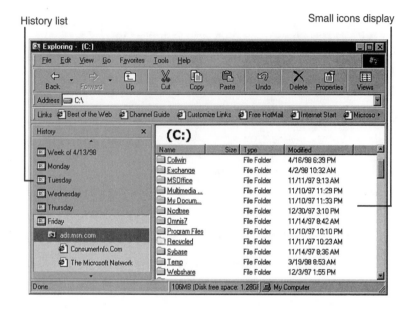

FIGURE 11.2   The Details view.

 Quick View   If the Standard Buttons toolbar is displayed, you can use its Views button to change views. Click Views button's down arrow, and select the file list view you want. (If the Standard Buttons toolbar isn't displayed, see the section "Working with Toolbars" for help.)

Normally, file extensions such as .DOC, .TXT, .BAT, and so on, do not appear in the file list. If you want to see the extensions, open the View menu, select Folder Options, and click the View tab. Then select the Hide file extensions for known file types option. To display hidden files (such as system files like WIN.INI, AUTOEXEC.BAT, and so on), select the Show all files option as well.

CONTROLLING THE ORDER OF THE FILE LIST DISPLAY

As shown in Figure 11.1, files are displayed in alphabetical order, with folders appearing at the top of the file list. To change the order of the list, follow these steps:

1. Open the View menu and select Arrange Icons.

2. Select the option you want from the cascading menu that appears: by Name, by Type, by Size, or by Date.

3. If you're using the Large Icons or Small Icons view, you can select the AutoArrange option to automatically arrange the icons in neat rows. (To arrange the icons one time, select the Line Up Icons command on the View menu.)

Fast Arrangement   If you're using the Details view, you can quickly sort the file list by any column by clicking that column's header. For example, click the Modified header to sort the files by date.

REPLACING THE ALL FOLDERS LIST

The All Folders list can be replaced with other Explorer Bar panels:

Search   Displays a Web page that lets you search the Internet. You'll learn how to perform searches in Lesson 25, "Searching for and Saving Web Page Locations."

Favorites   Displays a list of your favorite Internet sites. You add to this list just as you would within Internet Explorer; see Lesson 25 for help.

History   Displays a list of previous Internet sites you've visited. To visit a site, click it, and it's displayed in the file list window. The History list is displayed in Figure 11.2.

Channels   Displays a list of channels you can subscribe to. See Lesson 3, "Subscribing to Channels and Working Offline," for more information.

 Web Pages in Explorer?   In Windows 98, both My Computer and Explorer can be used as Web browsers of sorts. With the help of the Explorer Bar panels such as Search, Favorites, and History, you can quickly display your favorite Internet sites within the Explorer or the My Computer window.

To display the Explorer Bar panels in either My Computer or Explorer, open the View menu and select Explorer Bar. Then select the panel you want to display. (You cannot display the All Folders list in My Computer, but you can display any of the others listed here.)

PREVIEWING FILES

You can preview the contents of a file by right-clicking on it, then selecting Quick View from the shortcut menu. You can use this technique to view graphics files, Word document files, Excel worksheet files, and many other file types.

If you're viewing the folder as a Web page and you select a file, it is automatically previewed in the left panel. For example, if you select a graphics file, the graphic is displayed in the left panel, along with other file information such as the file size and date of last modification.

CUSTOMIZING FOLDERS IN WEB STYLE

When you select Web Style, the contents of your folders are displayed as Web pages, with icons representing each file or subfolder, as shown in Figure 11.3.

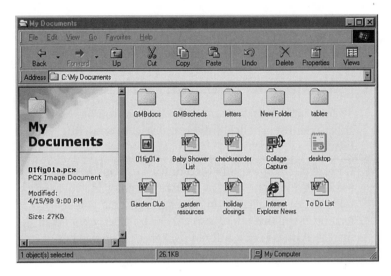

FIGURE 11.3 When you use Web Style, the contents of your folders look like Web pages.

A Web page gives you total freedom as to how you want your files organized and displayed within the folder.

If you don't want to go to the trouble of creating a Web page, you can simply display a graphic as a background for the folder. Although this option doesn't help you organize a folder's contents to suit your needs, it does allow you to add some spice to the display.

To create a Web page for your folder, follow these steps:

1. Open the View menu and select Customize this Folder.

2. Select Create or edit an HTML document. Click Next.

3. Windows prepares to start your HTML (Web page) editor. Click Next.

4. Make your changes to the Web page and save them. Then close your HTML editor.

5. Click Finish.

To add a graphic to the background of your folder, follow these steps:

1. Open the View menu and select Customize this Folder.

2. Select Choose a background picture. Click Next.

3. Select a bitmap graphic from the Background picture for this folder list, or click Browse and select your own bitmap.

4. If needed, change the Text color for the icons in the folder. (You might need to change the color in order for text to show up clearly on top of the graphic you selected.) If the text still doesn't show up clearly, you can display it on top of a colored Background (instead of directly on top of the graphic). Click Next.

5. Click Finish.

You can remove your customization for this folder by selecting the Remove customization option in the Customize this Folder dialog box.

WORKING WITH TOOLBARS

Both My Computer and Explorer come with several toolbars that let you work with your files more easily. Initially, the Standard Buttons toolbar is displayed, along with the Address and Links toolbars, as shown in Figure 11.4.

To display a toolbar, follow these steps:

1. Open the View menu and select Toolbars.

2. Select the toolbar you want to display from the cascading menu (currently displayed toolbars have a check mark next to them):

> **Standard Buttons** This toolbar provides file management commands such as copying and deleting. You'll learn the purpose of each of these buttons later in this lesson.

Address   This toolbar lets you type in an Internet address for display in the file list area. You can also select local addresses (such as a different drive) from the Address list.

Links   This toolbar provides quick access to popular locations on the Internet, such as Microsoft's home page.

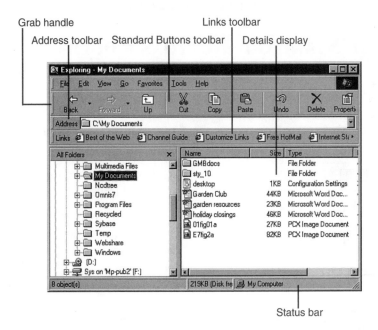

FIGURE 11.4   Toolbars provide quick access to common commands.

 No Words   To display only icons on the Standard Buttons toolbar (instead of icons and text), open the View menu, select Toolbars, and then select Text Labels.

To use a toolbar, click the button whose command you want to execute. To use the Address toolbar, click in its text box and type the address of the site you want to view, or select an address from the drop-down list.

To avoid crowding the toolbars on one line, you can display one toolbar under another, as shown in Figure 11.2. Click the toolbar's grab handle and drag it to its new location.

The Standard Buttons Toolbar

The Standard Buttons toolbar appears in both Explorer and My Computer. Table 11.1 lists each button and its purpose.

Table 11.1 The Buttons on the Standard Buttons Toolbar

Button	Name	Purpose
	Back	Redisplays a previously displayed folder.
	Forward	After you use Back, this button displays the original folder.
	Up	Moves up one level in the folder hierarchy.
	Cut	Moves the selected file or folder to the Clipboard.
	Copy	Copies the selected file or folder.
	Paste	Copies the file or folder from the Clipboard to the current location.
	Undo	Undoes the last action.
	Delete	Deletes the selected file or folder.

Button	Name	Purpose
	Properties	Displays the properties of the selected file or folder.
	Views	Lets you change the file list display.

In this lesson, you learned how to change the My Computer and Explorer file displays. You learned how to sort files and how to display them in Web pages. You also learned how to use the My Computer and Explorer toolbars. In the next lesson, you'll learn how to copy and move your files and folders.

Selecting, Copying, and Moving Files and Folders

In this lesson, you'll learn how to copy and move files and folders.

Selecting Multiple Files and Folders

Before you can copy or move a file or folder, you must select it. When you select a file or folder, it becomes highlighted. You can select more than one file or folder at a time in order to move or copy multiple files or folders in one step.

To select a file or folder, do the following:

- Click the file or folder you want to select.

- If you have the Web Style option turned on, point at the file you want to select. After a second or so, the file is highlighted so that you'll know it's selected.

To select contiguous files or folders (files or folders listed next to each other; see Figure 12.1), do one of the following:

- Click the first file or folder in the list, and then press and hold the Shift key as you click the last file you want to select.

- If you're using the Web Style option, point at the first file or folder you want to select and then press and hold the Shift key as you point to the last file you want to select.

Noncontiguous files   Contiguous files

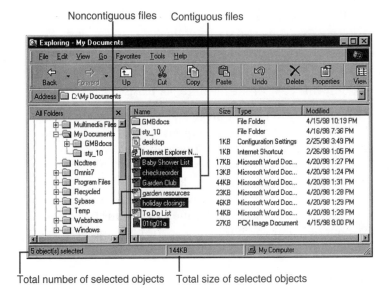

FIGURE 12.1   You can select multiple files or folders to copy or move.

To select noncontiguous files or folders (files or folders that are *not* listed next to each other; see Figure 12.1), do one of the following:

- Click the first file or folder you want to select, and then press and hold the Ctrl key as you click each additional file or folder.

- If you're using the Web Style option, point at the first file or folder you want to select, and then press and hold the Ctrl key as you point to each additional file or folder.

COPYING AND MOVING FILES AND FOLDERS

Once the files or folders you want to work with are selected, you can copy or move them as needed. When you copy a file or a folder, the original file or folder remains as is, and a copy is placed in the location you choose. Thus, two copies of the file or folder exist.

When you move a file or folder, it is deleted from its original location and then placed in the new location you select. In this scenario, only one copy of the file or folder exists.

The simplest way to copy or move a file or folder is to use *drag and drop*. Basically, you drag the objects to their new location and then drop them where you want them. In order to drag and drop successfully, you must be able to see within the My Computer or Explorer window both the original location of the file or folder *and* the location to which you want to copy or move it. (See Figure 12.2.) If you can't see both locations, you can still copy or move your files, but you'll want to use the copy and paste or cut and paste method, as explained later in this section.

Current folder appears open in the listing

Contents of original folder are displayed here

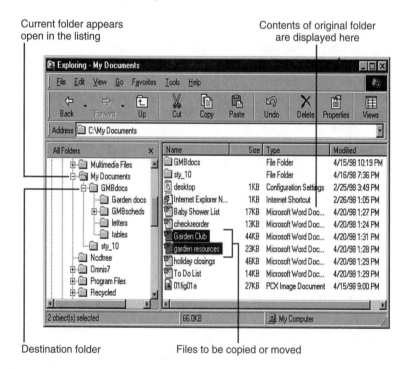

Destination folder

Files to be copied or moved

Figure 12.2 To make drag and drop easier, make sure both the original location and the destination location are visible.

For Easy Drag and Drop, Use Explorer   Since you can display the file hierarchy in Explorer's All Folders list, it's easy to arrange things so that you can see both the original and the final location of your files. I recommend using Explorer when attempting to drag and drop files to copy or move them.

COPYING FILES AND FOLDERS

To copy a file or folder, follow these steps:

1. Select the file(s) or folder(s) you want to copy.

2. Start dragging the file(s) or folder(s) to their new location. Before dropping them at the new location, press and hold down the Ctrl key.

3. Release the mouse button first, and then the Ctrl key.

 Already There?   If the file already exists in the location you're trying to copy it to, you'll see a warning telling you so. You can overwrite the existing file with the copy by clicking Yes.

If neither the original nor the destination location is visible, you can follow these steps to copy your files or folders:

1. Select the file(s) or folder(s) you want to copy.

2. Click the Copy button on the Standard Buttons toolbar, or open the Edit menu and select Copy.

3. Select the folder or drive you want to copy to.

4. Click the Paste button or open the Edit menu and select Paste.

MOVING FILES AND FOLDERS

To move a file or a folder, follow these steps:

1. Select the file(s) or folder(s) you want to move.

2. Start draging the file(s) or folder(s) to their new location. Before dropping them at the new location, press and hold down the Shift key.

3. Release the mouse button first, then the Shift key.

Drag and Drop Methods If you're moving files to *the same drive*—for example, from a folder on drive C to another folder on drive C, you don't have to hold down the Shift key as you drag. In addition, if you're copying files from one drive to another, you don't need to hold down the Ctrl key.

If neither the original nor the destination location is visible, you can follow these steps to move your files or folders:

1. Select the file(s) or folder(s) you want to move.

2. Click the Cut button on the Standard Buttons toolbar, or open the Edit menu and select Cut.

3. Select the folder or drive you want to move to.

4. Click the Paste button or open the Edit menu and select Paste.

Oops! If you copy or move the wrong files or folders, you can undo your mistake by clicking the Undo button on the Standard Buttons toolbar or by opening the Edit menu and selecting Undo.

THE RIGHT-DRAG METHOD

Another way to quickly place files where you want them is with the right-drag method. The advantage of this method is that it works the same whether you're copying or moving files:

1. Select the files you want to move or copy.

2. Point to the files and click and hold down the *right* mouse button.

3. Drag the files where you want them and release the mouse button. A shortcut menu appears. From there, you can select the Copy or Move command as needed.

CREATING SHORTCUTS

Rather than actually copying or moving a file into another folder, you can create a shortcut to it. A *shortcut* is an icon that points to the real file, wherever it might actually be. Shortcuts are used to open files and programs without having to select them from the Start menu or from their permanent location on the hard disk. You'll find most shortcuts on your Desktop, although they can exist anywhere.

To create a shortcut, follow the steps in the preceding section for right-dragging: Select the file you want to create a shortcut to, click and hold down the right mouse button and then drag the file to its final destination. When you release the mouse button, select Create Shortcut(s) Here from the pop-up menu that appears.

Shortcuts, by the way, appear as normal icons, except that they also have a tiny bent arrow in their bottom-left corner. This arrow tells you that the icon is a shortcut and not an actual file. Thus, you can safely delete a shortcut icon without accidentally deleting any real file.

To use your shortcut, double-click (or click) it. The program associated with that file opens automatically.

USING SEND TO

If you often copy files to a disk or to a particular folder, you can use the Send To menu option to perform that task more quickly.

To use the Send To menu option, follow these steps:

1. Select the file(s) or folder(s) you want to send.

2. Open the File menu and select the Send To command.

3. Select the destination for the file(s) or folder(s) from the Send To menu.

The Send To menu option contains these destinations:

Floppy drives   This command lets you copy files to available diskette drives.

Desktop as Shortcut   If you send a file to the Desktop, it appears as a shortcut icon. You can then open the file by clicking (or double-clicking) it.

Mail Recipient   This command lets you create a quick email message with the file you select attached to it.

My Briefcase   This command places the file in your Briefcase, for eventual transfer to your laptop PC.

My Documents   This command moves the file to the My Documents folder.

You can add your own destinations to this menu. Follow these steps:

1. Select the destination you want to add. For example, select the folder you want to add to the menu.

2. Press and hold down the *right* mouse button as you drag the folder to the Send To folder (which is located within the Windows folder on your hard drive).

3. Select Create Shortcut(s) Here from the shortcut menu that appears.

In this lesson, you learned how to select, copy, and move files and folders. You also learned how to use the Send To menu option to save time. In the next lesson, you'll learn how to create, rename, delete, and find files and folders.

13

CREATING, DELETING, RENAMING, AND FINDING FILES AND FOLDERS

In this lesson, you'll learn how to create, delete, rename, and find files and folders.

CREATING A FOLDER

Windows 98 provides a My Documents folder for your data files, but you might prefer to organize your files by creating subfolders within the My Documents folder. Alternatively, you might want to create your own folders somewhere else on your hard drive.

Here's how to create a new folder:

1. Select the drive on which you want to place your new folder. To create a subfolder, select the folder into which you want your new folder placed. For example, select the My Documents folder to create a subfolder for it.

2. Open the File menu and select New.

3. Select New Folder from the cascading menu that appears. A folder is created in the current directory.

4. Type a name for the folder and press Enter. You can give the folder any name, up to 255 characters long, including spaces.

DELETING A FILE OR FOLDER

When you delete a file or folder, it's placed in the Recycle Bin. This gives you a chance to get an accidentally deleted file back. You'll learn how to use the Recycle Bin in the next section. When you delete a folder, you delete all files contained in it, as well as the folder itself.

 Insurance Policy   Even with the Recycle Bin, it's possible to still lose a file. So you might want to back up your files to disks before you delete them. See Lesson 23, "Disk Management," for help.

To delete a file or folder, follow these steps:

1. Select the file(s) or folder(s) you want to delete.

2. Click the Delete button on the Standard Buttons toolbar, or press the Delete key on the keyboard. The Confirm File Delete dialog box appears.

3. Click Yes to delete the file(s) or folder(s).

 I Didn't Mean to Delete That!   If you notice right away you've made a mistake deleting a file or folder, click the Undo button on the Standard Buttons toolbar or open the Edit menu and select Undo to restore the file. Otherwise, read the next section to learn how to retrieve your file or folder.

EMPTYING THE RECYCLE BIN

Once a file or folder is sent to the Recycle Bin, it stays there until you empty it. This helps prevent the deletion of files when you exit Windows.

To retrieve a file or folder from the Recycle Bin, follow these steps:

1. Open the Recycle Bin, shown in Figure 13.1, by clicking
(or double-clicking) it. You'll find an icon for the Recycle
Bin on the Desktop.

FIGURE 13.1 Deleted items are moved to the Recycle Bin.

2. Select the items you want to restore.

3. Open the File menu and select Restore. The items you
selected are restored to their original locations.

 Not All Files   The Recycle Bin can't be used to restore
files that were deleted from a disk. These files aren't
saved to the Recycle Bin. So be careful when removing
files from a disk.

Now, because you might have deleted several files or folders to
make more room on your hard disk, and because all those deleted
files and folders were actually moved to the Recycle Bin and not
really removed from the hard disk, you'll need to empty the Recycle Bin to gain extra hard disk space.

To empty the Recycle Bin, follow these steps:

1. Open the Recycle Bin.

2. Open the File menu and select Empty Recycle Bin. Or, if the Recycle Bin is displayed as a Web page, click the Empty Recycle Bin link.

If you want to remove only one or two items from the Recycle Bin, you can. Just select them and click the Delete button on the Standard Buttons toolbar, or press the Delete key on the keyboard.

 Empty It Quickly   You can actually empty the Recycle Bin without opening it. Right-click the Recycle Bin icon and select Empty Recycle Bin from the shortcut menu that appears.

BYPASSING THE RECYCLE BIN

You can delete files or folders without sending them to the Recycle Bin. This saves you the step of emptying the Bin later to actually get rid of the files. However, it also removes your "safety net." Here's what to do:

1. Select the file or folder you want to permanently delete.

2. Right-click to bring up the shortcut menu.

3. Press and hold down the Shift key.

4. Select Delete from the shortcut menu.

5. Click Yes to confirm.

You can turn off the Recycle Bin for all your file deletions if you want, although it might be dangerous to do so, since you'll have no way to restore accidentally deleted files. To turn off the Recycle Bin, right-click its icon on the desktop and select Properties from the shortcut menu. Select the Do not move files to the Recycle Bin option and click OK.

RENAMING FILES AND FOLDERS

You might want to rename a file or folder if it turns out that the original name you chose doesn't clearly identify the purpose of the file or folder. To rename a file or folder, follow these steps:

1. Select the file or folder you want to rename. (You can rename only one object at a time.)

2. Open the File menu and select Rename.

3. Type the new name for the selected file or folder and press Enter. Be sure to type the same file extension as before. For example, if the filename ended in .DOC, be sure to use .DOC at the end of the filename you type.

If you're using the Classic style (single-click) option, you can click a file to select it and then click the filename portion of the icon to rename it. The second time you click the file, a cursor appears in the filename. Make changes as needed, and then press Enter to save the new filename.

SEARCHING FOR A FILE

With the large hard drives in use today, it's easy to lose track of a single file. In Explorer (not My Computer) you can search for your lost files by entering a complete or partial name, the date the file was created, the file type, or the file's size. You can even look for some matching text within the file.

If you're unsure of the exact spelling of a filename, you can use wildcards when entering a filename to search for. There are two wildcards you can use: an asterisk represents multiple characters, and a question mark represents a single character in the filename. Table 13.1 lists some sample uses of wildcards.

TABLE 13.1   EXAMPLES OF WILDCARD USE

WILDCARD ENTERED	SEARCH RESULTS
sales*.doc	sales95.doc, sales 96.doc, sales.97.doc
sales.*	sales.doc, sales.xls, sales.ppt

WILDCARD ENTERED	SEARCH RESULTS
sales?.doc	sales1.doc, sales2.doc, sales3.doc
sales??.doc	sales11.doc, sales12.doc
sa*.xls	sailing.xls, sales97.xls, sam.xls
sa*.*	sailing.xls, sales97.doc, sam.ppt

To search for a file or folder, follow these steps:

1. In Explorer, open the Tools menu and select Find. Then select Files or Folders from the cascading menu that appears. The Find: All Files dialog box appears, as shown in Figure 13.2.

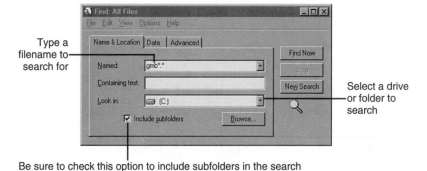

FIGURE 13.2 Searching for a lost file.

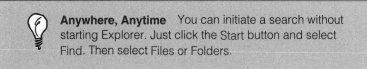

Anywhere, Anytime You can initiate a search without starting Explorer. Just click the Start button and select Find. Then select Files or Folders.

2. Type the name you want to search for in the Named text box. You can use wildcards if you like. If you've searched for this file recently, you can select it from the drop-down list box.

3. If you want to search for a file that contains a particular phrase, type that phrase in the Containing text text box.

4. Select the folder in which you want to search from the Look in drop-down list box, or click Browse to select it from a list. To search a drive, such as drive C:, select it instead. To search an entire drive, make sure that the Include subfolders option is selected.

5. To search for a file with a particular creation date or last modification date, click the Date tab. Then select the date options you want.

6. To search for a file of a particular type or size, click the Advanced tab and select the options you need.

7. When you're through selecting options, click Find Now. The results appear in a window under the Find dialog box, as shown in Figure 13.3.

Results

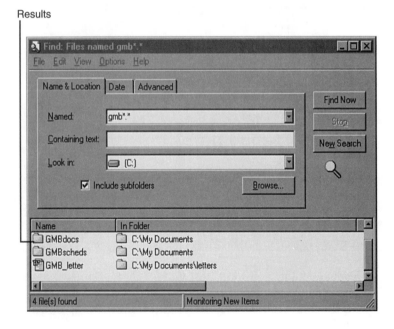

FIGURE 13.3 The results of your search.

8. If you didn't get the results you wanted, you can modify your search criteria and click Find Now again. Or, to erase the criteria and start over, click New Search.

You can also use the Find command to locate people and sites on the Internet. See Lesson 25, "Searching for and Saving Web Page Locations," for help.

In this lesson, you learned how to create and delete files and folders. You also learned how to rename files and search for them. In the next lesson, you'll learn how to format, name, and make copies of floppy disks.

14 Formatting, Naming, and Copying Floppy Disks

In this lesson, you'll learn how to maintain your floppy disks. You'll learn how to judge the remaining space on a disk, how to format a disk, and how to make a copy of an existing disk.

How to Tell How Much Room Is on a Disk

Even though disks today contain much more space than old-style disks, they are limited as to how much they can hold. So before you decide to use a disk to store a particular set of files, you might want to see how much room is on the disk. You can use the same steps to determine the amount of space left on your hard disk.

To see how much room is on a disk, follow these steps:

1. Within Explorer or My Computer, select My Computer from the Address drop-down list box or from the All Folders list.

2. Select the drive whose space you want to determine. If you use Web Style, the capacity also appears as a graph on the left side of the window, as shown in Figure 14.1.

You can also view a graph by selecting the drive and clicking the Properties button on the Standard Buttons toolbar. The Properties graph, shown in Figure 14.2, displays the exact amount of free space (not rounded up, as it is in the graph shown in Figure 14.1). This dialog box also provides access to tools you can use to rename the disk, check for errors and correct them, check the backup status of files on the disk, permit disk sharing, and compress the disk.

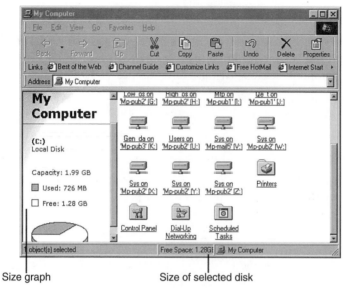

Size graph   Size of selected disk

FIGURE 14.1   The graph lets you quickly assess the remaining space on a disk.

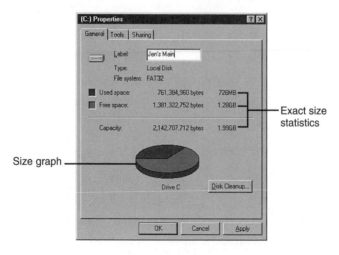

Size graph

Exact size statistics

FIGURE 14.2   The Properties graph.

FORMATTING A FLOPPY DISK

Before you can use a disk for the first time, it must be formatted. Formatting is a process that divides the disk into segments that the computer uses to store (and later, to locate) data on the disk.

Most disks you buy today are already formatted, but you might want to reformat a disk to erase its contents or to check for errors on the disk.

To format a disk, follow these steps:

1. In Explorer or My Computer, select My Computer from the Address drop-down list box or from the All Folders list.

2. Select the drive you want to format.

3. Open the File menu and select Format. The Format dialog box, shown in Figure 14.3, appears.

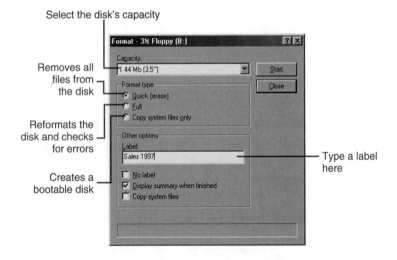

FIGURE 14.3   To prepare a disk for use, format it.

Quicker Formatting Another way to format a disk is to right-click it within the All Folders panel and select Format from the shortcut menu that appears.

4. Double-check the Capacity, and if needed, select the correct capacity from the drop-down list.

5. Select the type of format you want to perform from the Format type list. If you're having problems with your disk, select Full.

6. Type a label for the disk (up to 11 characters), such as **Work Files**. If you don't want to use a label, select that option.

7. Normally, a summary is displayed when the formatting process is over; this allows you to verify that everything went well. If you don't want to display this summary, uncheck the Display summary when finished option to turn it off.

8. If you're formatting a new disk and you want to make it bootable, select the Copy system files option.

 Bootable A bootable disk is one that can be used to start your system if something happens to the startup files on the hard disk. You should have at least one bootable disk for emergencies.

9. When you're ready, click Start to begin the formatting process. When it's done, a summary is displayed. After viewing the summary, click Close.

10. You can format additional disks by repeating steps 4 through 9. When you're through, click the Close button (×).

COPYING A DISK

You can make an exact copy of a disk whenever you need to. Use the copy for everyday tasks, and keep the original in a safe place. This can help ensure that your data won't get lost if some of your disks become damaged.

To make a copy of a disk, you'll need another disk of the exact same size and capacity. *You can't make a copy of one size of disk onto a disk of another size or capacity.* Usually, you use only a single disk drive to copy disks, swapping disks halfway through the process, although you can use two different drives, provided that they're the same type.

Follow these steps:

1. Insert the disk you want to copy into its drive.

2. In Explorer or My Computer, select My Computer from the Address drop-down list box or from the All Folders list.

3. Select the floppy disk you want to make a copy of.

4. Open the File menu and select Copy Disk. The Copy Disk dialog box, shown in Figure 14.4, appears.

FIGURE 14.4 Make copies of important disks.

5. Select the drive you want to Copy from and Copy to, and then click Start.

6. Insert the disk you want to copy to, and click OK.

7. If you have another disk to copy, insert it into its drive and repeat steps 3 through 6. When you're through, click Close.

In this lesson, you learned how to determine the amount of space on a disk. You also learned how to format and copy disks. In the next lesson, you'll learn how to install and remove applications.

15 LESSON

INSTALLING AND UNINSTALLING WINDOWS 98 APPLICATIONS

In this lesson, you'll learn how to install and remove your applications.

INSTALLING SOFTWARE

Most applications today come with their own installation programs, so installing software is a fairly simple process. But before you start, check these items:

- First, make sure you exit any programs you might be running. Because most installation programs make changes to your system files, exiting your programs will prevent any conflicts from occurring. In addition, you might need to restart your computer during the installation, so exiting your programs prevents any possible loss of data.

- If you're upgrading your software to a newer version, be sure to make copies of all your existing data, in case something happens to it during the upgrade process. Also, be aware that some programs (but certainly not the majority) require you to uninstall the previous version before upgrading. Most, however, allow you to upgrade on top of the existing software. Read the installation manual before proceeding.

To install a program, follow these basic steps:

1. Insert the first installation disk (or the CD-ROM) into its drive. Many programs that are distributed on CD-ROM

will automatically start their installation when the CD-ROM is placed in the drive. If so, you can skip to step 4.

2. Click the Start button and select Run.

3. Type the path and the filename of the installation program and click OK. For example, to install a program from drive A:, you might type something like **A:SETUP** or **A:INSTALL**. (Check with the installation manual for the exact command you need to type.) Or you can click the Browse button and locate the setup file yourself.

4. At this point, the installation program will prompt you to make whatever selections are needed. For example, you might be asked to select the drive and folder into which you want the program installed. If you're upgrading over a prior version, make sure you select the directory in which it was originally installed. Continue to follow the onscreen prompts until the program is installed.

Many installations offer a choice as to the type of setup you can select. For example, you might be offered the choices Compact, Typical, and Custom. Compact in this case would offer you a slimmed-down version of the program (a good choice if you're short on hard disk space), while Typical installs all the basic options. Custom lets you select the options you want (and those you don't want).

The installation program will create whatever folders are needed. After checking to make sure there is enough space, it will then copy the contents of the installation disks or CD-ROM to your hard disk. It will also add a command for starting the program to your Start menu.

UNINSTALLING SOFTWARE

If you've decided that you no longer need a particular program, you should remove it from the hard disk to make room for the programs you do use. Follow these steps:

1. Click the Start button and select Settings. Then select Control Panel from the shortcut menu that appears.

2. Click (or double-click) the Add/Remove Programs icon. The Add/Remove Programs Properties dialog box appears, as shown in Figure 15.1.

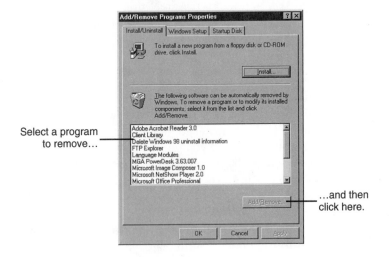

Select a program to remove...

...and then click here.

Figure 15.1   Removing unwanted programs from the hard disk.

3. Select the program you want to delete and click Add/Remove.

4. You may be prompted to insert the installation disk or CD-ROM for the program you're removing. Do so and then click OK.

5. Your application's uninstall program starts. Follow the onscreen prompts to remove the program from your hard disk.

In this lesson, you learned how to install and uninstall a program on your computer. In the next lesson, you'll learn how to use your applications.

USING WINDOWS 98 APPLICATIONS

*In this lesson, you'll learn how to use
your Windows applications: how to start them; how to copy and move
information; and how to open, close, and save your documents.*

STARTING A WINDOWS APPLICATION

To use an application, you must start it. When a program is installed, a command to start it is placed on the Start menu. To
access the proper command, click the Start button, select Programs, and then select the folder in which the program's start
command is stored. (See Figure 16.1.) There are several other ways
in which you can start programs:

Programs menu

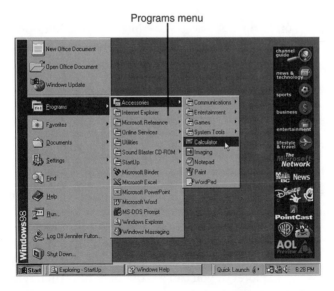

FIGURE 16.1 Programs are stored in their own folder.

- **With the Run command**   If the program you want to
  start doesn't have a command on the Start menu, click
  the Start button and select Run. Click Browse, select the
  path of the ezzxecutable file (.EXE) for the program, and
  click OK.

- **By file association**   When a program is installed, it
  registers the types of files that can be created with it. You
  can then use these file associations to start the program
  with a particular document. For example, if you select a
  file with a .DOC extension within My Computer or Explorer, you can open the document and start Microsoft
  Word at the same time. Double-click a file, and the associated program will start.

- **With the Documents or Favorites menu**   The documents you've worked on most recently are displayed on
  the Documents menu. You can use it to start the associated program with the selected document open and ready
  for you to work on. In addition, you can save documents
  to the Favorites or the My Documents folders and access
  them through the Start menu. Just click the Start button,
  select Documents or Favorites, and select the document
  you want to open. To access documents in the My Documents folder, select it after selecting Favorites.

- **When you start Windows**   You can select certain
  programs and have Windows start them for you automatically when you start your computer. Just right-click a
  program's startup file and then drag it into the Startup
  folder (which you'll find in the \Windows\Start
  Menu\Programs folder). Then select Create Shortcut(s)
  Here from the menu that appears.

- **With a shortcut icon**   You can create an icon for your
  program and place it on the Desktop. Then, to start the
  program, all you need to do is double-click the icon. To
  create a shortcut, right-click the program's start file, and
  then drag the file out onto the Desktop (you might have
  to resize Explorer so you can see the Desktop). Then select
  Create Shortcut(s) Here from the menu that appears.

• **With the Quick Launch toolbar**   You can drag an application's start file (.EXE file) to the Quick Launch toolbar on the taskbar to create an icon. You can then click this icon to start the program.

CREATING AND OPENING DOCUMENTS

After starting your Windows application, you might want to begin a new document or open an existing one.

To begin a new document, open the program's File menu and select New. You might need to make additional selections if your program can create more than one type of new document.

To open an existing document, open the program's File menu and select Open. The Open dialog box appears. For most programs, it will look something like Figure 16.2. Select the folder in which your document is located from the Look in drop-down list box. Then select your document from those listed and click Open.

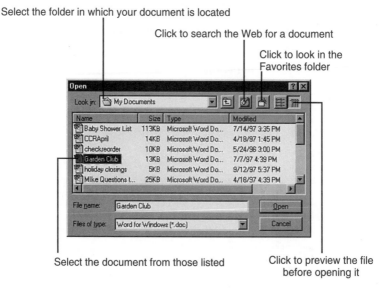

Select the folder in which your document is located

Click to search the Web for a document

Click to look in the Favorites folder

Select the document from those listed

Click to preview the file before opening it

FIGURE 16.2   You must open a document if you want to make changes to it.

If the document you want to open is a recent one, you'll find it listed at the bottom of the program's File menu. Simply open the File menu and select the document you want to open from those listed at the bottom of the menu.

Many programs let you open several documents at one time and switch between them as needed. First, open as many documents as you need. Then open the program's Window menu and select the document you want to switch to from those listed.

Copying and Moving Information

When you copy or move data, it's first placed on the Clipboard. The Clipboard is a kind of "holding area" for the data while the copy or move operation is being carried out. The Clipboard is a part of Windows, and not the program, so you can easily use it to copy or move data between *applications* as well as between documents within an application.

Selecting Text and Graphics

Before beginning a copy or move operation, you must select the item you want to work with. The item you select appears highlighted, so you can easily distinguish it from unselected objects.

To select text, you drag over it:

1. Click at the beginning of the text you want to select.

2. Press and hold down the mouse button as you drag over the text you want to select. The text is highlighted, as shown in Figure 16.3.

Shortcut to Selection   Most programs support the use of these shortcuts when selecting text: To select a word, double-click it. To select a paragraph, double-click in the left margin.

To select a graphic, click it. Small boxes, called *handles,* appear around the graphic to show that it's highlighted, as shown in Figure 16.4.

Selected text

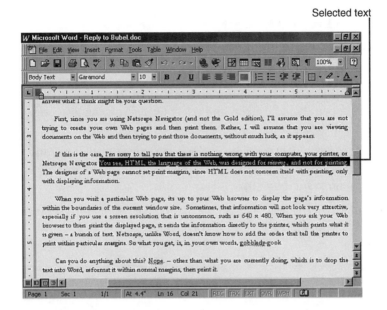

FIGURE 16.3 Selected text is highlighted in reverse video.

Handles

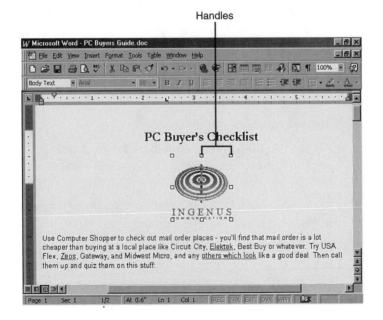

FIGURE 16.4 When you select a graphic, handles appear.

Copying Data

To copy data, follow these steps:

1. Select the data you want to copy.

2. Click the Copy button on the toolbar (if there is one) or open the Edit menu and select Copy. You can also press Ctrl+C.

3. Click in the spot where you want the data copied. You can switch to another document, and even to another program if you like.

4. Click the Paste button on the toolbar, or open the Edit menu and select Paste. You can also press Ctrl+V.

 Let's Do That Again!   When data is copied or moved, it's placed on the Clipboard, where it remains until it's replaced by some new item to be copied or moved. This means that if you repeat the Paste command, the same data can be copied (or moved) to multiple locations.

Moving Data

To move data, follow these steps:

1. Select the data you want to move.

2. Click the Cut button on the toolbar (if there is one) or open the Edit menu and select Cut. You can also press Ctrl+X.

3. Click in the spot where you want the data moved. Again, you can switch to another document, and even to another program if you want to.

4. Click the Paste button on the toolbar, or open the Edit menu and select Paste. You can also press Ctrl+V.

Drag and Drop   You can drag and drop your data to copy or move it: Select the data you want to copy or move, and then drag the data to its new location. *When copying, be sure to press and hold down the Ctrl key as you drag.* Release the mouse button, and the data is copied or moved.

SAVING AND CLOSING DOCUMENTS

After you're through working on a document, you should close it to free up system resources for other applications. Before closing a document, you need to save it so you won't lose any changes you've made.

To save a document, follow these steps:

1. Click the Save button on the toolbar (if there is one), or open the File menu and select Save. If this is the first time you've saved the file, the Save As dialog box, similar to the one shown in Figure 16.5, appears. (This dialog box will *not* appear the next time you save this same file.)

Select a folder to save the file in

Type a
filename
here

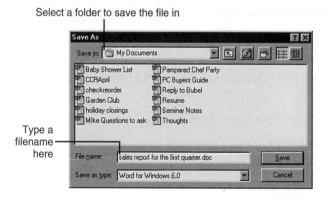

FIGURE 16.5   The Save As dialog box.

2. Select the folder in which you want your document saved from the Save in drop-down list box.

 The Place to Save   Using one folder can make it easy to keep track of all your documents. Microsoft programs all default to a common folder called the My Documents folder. You might prefer to save this particular document in the Favorites folder (which you can get to by clicking the Look in Favorites button). Documents in both the My Documents and the Favorites folders are easily accessible from the Start menu.

3. Type a name for the file in the File name text box. The name can contain up to 255 characters (including spaces).

4. Click Save.

After you save a document, it remains open so that you can continue working on it. If you make additional changes, save them by clicking the Save button or opening the File menu and selecting Save.

To close a document, open the File menu and select Close. If the document contains changes that haven't yet been saved, you'll be prompted to save them.

EXITING A WINDOWS APPLICATION

Before you exit an application, you should save your open documents. Then, to exit the application, do one of the following:

- **Use the File menu**   Open the program's File menu and select Exit. If you have any open documents that haven't been saved yet, you'll be asked if you'd like to save them.

- **Use the program's Close button**   You can also click the program's Close button (x) to exit a program.

- **Use the keyboard shortcut**   If you prefer to use the keyboard, you can press Alt+F4 to close the program's window and thus exit the program.

In this lesson, you learned how to start and exit your applications; how to open, close, and save documents; and how to copy or move data. In the next lesson, you'll learn how to use WordPad.

17

CREATING A DOCUMENT WITH WORDPAD

In this lesson, you'll learn how to use WordPad to create text documents.

CREATING AND EDITING A DOCUMENT

WordPad is a basic word processing program that you can use to create letters, memos, reports, and other documents. To create a document with WordPad, select Start | Programs | Accessories and then start typing. To create another new document later, click the New button on the toolbar, as shown in Figure 17.1.

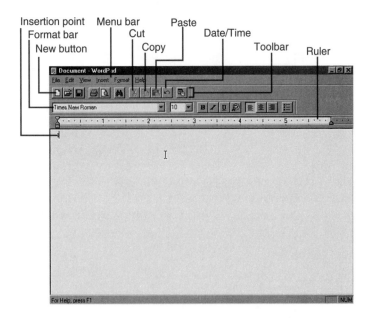

FIGURE 17.1 Creating a new document with WordPad is simple.

TYPING TEXT

When typing text into your document, remember these tips:

Text is inserted at the *insertion point*. To move the insertion point, click in the document at some other point. You can also move the insertion point using the keyboard. To type over existing text, switch to Overtype mode. To do so, press the Insert key. What you type replaces existing text, beginning at the insertion point. To switch back to normal (insertion) mode, press the Insert key again.

To erase a mistake, press the Backspace key. Characters to the left of the insertion point are deleted. If you press the Delete key instead, characters to the *right* of the insertion point are deleted. You can also select text and press the Delete key to remove it.

To select text, click at the beginning of the text you want to select and then drag over the text to highlight it. You can select text with the keyboard by pressing and holding down the Shift key as you use the arrow keys to highlight text.

To move the insertion point with the keyboard, use the keys listed in Table 17.1.

TABLE 17.1   KEYS YOU CAN USE TO MOVE THE INSERTION POINT

KEY OR KEY COMBINATION	DESCRIPTION
Arrow key	Moves up or down one line, or left or right one character.
Page Up or Page Down	Moves to the previous screen or the next screen.
Ctrl+left arrow or Ctrl+right arrow	Moves left or right one word.
Ctrl+Page Up or Ctrl+Page Down	Moves to the top or bottom of the screen.

continues

TABLE 17.1 CONTINUED

KEY OR KEY COMBINATION	DESCRIPTION
Home or End	Moves to the beginning or end of the line.
Ctrl+Home	Moves to the beginning of the document.
Ctrl+End	Moves to the end of the document.

 Inserting the Date You can quickly insert the date into a document (rather than typing it) by clicking the Date/Time button on the toolbar. Select a format and click OK.

COPYING AND MOVING TEXT

After text is selected, copying or moving it is a simple process:

To copy text, follow these steps:

1. Select the text you want to copy.

2. Click the Copy button on the toolbar.

3. Move the insertion point to the location where you would like to copy the text.

4. Click the Paste button on the toolbar.

To move text, follow these steps:

1. Select the text you want to move.

2. Click the Cut button on the toolbar.

3. Move the insertion point to the location where you would like to move the text.

4. Click the Paste button on the toolbar.

You can also use drag and drop to copy or move text. Select the text you want to move, and then drag it to its new location. To copy the text instead, press and hold down the Ctrl key as you drag.

FORMATTING A DOCUMENT

After typing text into your document, you can change its appearance to emphasize your words. You can change the text's font, font style (the text's attributes, such as bold and italic), and font size. See Figure 17.2.

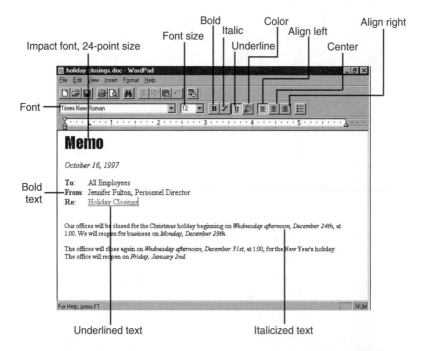

FIGURE 17.2   Formatting lets you change the look of your text.

 Font   A set of characters that have the same typeface, or text style. Times New Roman is the default font used in Word-Pad. You can change your text to another font as needed.

CHANGING THE FONT, FONT STYLE, AND FONT SIZE OF TEXT

To change the text's format, follow these steps:

1. Select the text you want to change.

2. Select the font you want to use from the Font drop-down list box on the Formatting toolbar.

3. To change the size of the selected text, select the size you want from the Font Size drop-down list box on the Formatting toolbar.

 Point Size   Text size is measured in points. A point is $1/72$ of an inch.

---

4. To apply a font style, click the appropriate button on the Formatting toolbar, such as Bold, Italic, Underline, or Color.

If you need to change several attributes of your selected text, you might prefer to use the Font dialog box. To display it, open the Format menu and select Font.

MODIFYING TEXT ALIGNMENT

Normally, text is left-aligned, meaning that it's placed against the left margin. You can change your text's alignment. For example, you can make a heading centered. Here's how:

1. Click anywhere inside the paragraph you want to align.

2. Click the appropriate button on the Formatting toolbar: Align Left, Center, or Align Right.

ADJUSTING PAGE MARGINS, PAPER SIZE, AND ORIENTATION

By default, WordPad documents are set up for printing on 8$^1/_2$-inch-by-11-inch paper, with left and right margins of 1$^1/_2$ inches. You can change these margins, and the top and bottom margins as well, with the Page Setup dialog box. You can also select a different paper size on which to print. In addition, you can change the *page orientation*.

 Page Orientation Selecting Portrait orientation causes the text to be printed across the shortest width of the paper. Landscape orientation prints text across the page's longest width.

To change the paper size, margins, or page orientation of your document, follow these steps:

1. Open the File menu and select Page Setup. The Page Setup dialog box, shown in Figure 17.3, appears.

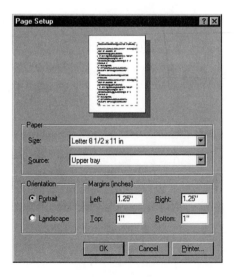

FIGURE 17.3 Changing the paper size, margins, and orientation.

2. Select a different paper size if needed from the Size drop-down list box.

3. To change the page orientation, select the option you want from the Orientation frame.

4. To change the page margins, click in the appropriate field (Left, Right, Top, or Bottom) and type the margin you want to use.

5. Click OK when you're through.

In this lesson, you learned how to use the WordPad accessory to create text documents. In the next lesson, you'll learn how to use Paint to create graphic images.

CREATING GRAPHICS WITH PAINT

In this lesson, you'll learn how to use Paint to create graphic images.

DRAWING IN PAINT

With the Paint accessory, shown in Figure 18.1, you can create colorful graphic images for use in your documents or as Windows wallpaper. You can start Paint by selecting Start | Programs | Accessories.

Tool box

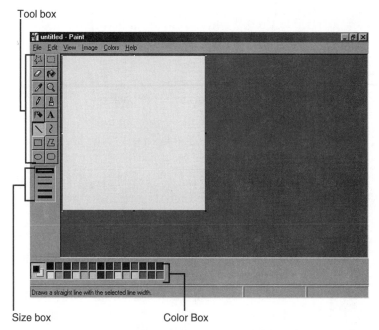

Size box   Color Box

FIGURE 18.1   Paint is ready for you to create your graphic.

To create your image, you use the tools in the Tool Box. You can change the color of the objects you draw with the Color Box. (I'll explain more about the use of color in the next section.) You can also change the size of the lines you draw (and the size of the outline of drawn objects) with the Line Size box.

Here's how to use each tool:

 Free Form Select   Drag around the area you want to select.

 Select   Click at the upper-left corner of the area you want to select, and then drag down and to the right to select a rectangular area.

 Eraser   Drag over any part of the drawing you want to erase.

 Fill with Color   Click any part of the drawing, and that area is filled with the current foreground color.

 Pick Color   You can change the foreground color to any color in the drawing by clicking that portion of the drawing.

 Magnifier   Click to zoom that area of the drawing. Click the area again to zoom back out.

 Pencil   Drag to draw a freehand line. To draw a straight line, press and hold down the Shift key as you drag.

 Brush   Select the size of brush tip you want to use from the Size box. Then drag to brush the drawing with the current foreground color.

 Airbrush   Select the amount of spray you want from the Size box. Then drag to spray the drawing with the current foreground color.

 Text   Use this tool to add text to a drawing. I'll explain exactly how to do this in the section "Adding Text to a Graphic."

Line   Select the line width you want to use from the Size box. Then click where you'd like to place one end of the line and drag to draw the line. To create a horizontal or vertical line, press and hold down the Shift key as you drag.

 Curve   Select the line width you want from the Size box. Then click at the point where you want the curve to begin, and drag to create a straight line. Then, click where you want the line to curve, and drag outward to bend the line. Repeat to add another curve to the line if you wish. (A line can have no more than two curves.)

 Rectangle   Select from the Fill Style box whether you want a filled or unfilled rectangle. Click to establish the upper-left corner of the rectangle, and then drag downward and to the right until the rectangle is the size you want. To create a square, press and hold down the Shift key as you drag.

 Polygon   Select from the Fill Style box whether you want a filled or unfilled polygon. Click to establish the first corner of the polygon, and then drag to create the first side. Continue dragging to create each side in turn. Double-click when you're through drawing the polygon.

 Ellipse   Select from the Fill Style box whether you want a filled or unfilled ellipse. Click to establish the upper-left edge of the ellipse, and then drag downward and to the right until the ellipse is the size you need. To create a perfect circle, press and hold down the Shift key as you drag.

 Rounded Rectangle   Select from the Fill Style box whether you want a filled or unfilled rectangle. Click to establish the upper-left corner of the rectangle, then drag downward and to the right until the rectangle is the size you want. To create a square, press and hold down the Shift key as you drag.

Bad Drawing If you make a mistake while drawing an object, open the Edit menu and select Undo to remove it.

Adding Color and Fill

The lower-left corner of the Color Box, shown in Figure 18.2, contains two overlapping squares. The upper square indicates the foreground color, and the lower square determines the background color. In Paint, the foreground color is used for the outline of the object you draw, and the background color is used for the fill (that is, if you choose to draw a filled object). To change the foreground color, click a color in the Color Box. To change the background color, right-click instead.

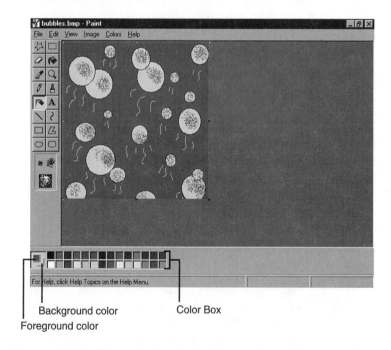

Figure 18.2 You can change the color of the objects you draw.

Before drawing an object such as a rounded rectangle, you can choose whether you want it to be filled or unfilled. Click the appropriate icon in the Fill Style box: Outline Only, Outline with Fill, or Fill Only.

 Switcheroo You can create an object that has an outline the color of the background and a fill with the color of the foreground by using the *right mouse button* when you draw the object.

ADDING TEXT TO A GRAPHIC

To add text to your drawing, you use the Text tool. Here's what to do:

1. Click the Text tool.

2. Select whether you want the background of your text box to be filled or unfilled by clicking the appropriate icon in the Fill Style box.

3. Click to establish the upper-left corner, and then drag downward to create a text box.

4. Use the Fonts toolbar to select the font, size, and text attributes you want to use.

5. Type your text. When you're through, click outside the text box.

 Be Careful of What You Type You can't go back and correct your text after you click outside the text box, so be sure it's correct.

In this lesson, you learned how to use the Paint accessory to create simple graphic images for use in your documents. In the next lesson, you'll learn how to use Windows multimedia accessories.

19

WORKING WITH SOUND AND VIDEO

In this lesson, you'll learn how to use Windows sound and video accessories.

USING THE CD PLAYER

With the CD Player, you can play audio CDs from your CD-ROM drive while you work with other applications. Follow these steps:

1. Insert a CD into the CD-ROM drive. The CD Player starts up minimized, and the music begins playing. When you click on the application's taskbar button, its main window appears, as shown in Figure 19.1.

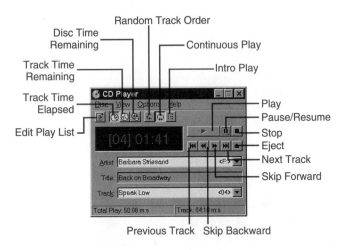

FIGURE 19.1 The CD Player plays audio CDs.

2. The music begins playing. To pause the playback, click the Pause button. Click it again to resume. You can click other buttons as well, as shown in Figure 19.1.

3. Use the toolbar buttons to control the playback and display (if the toolbar is not displayed, open the View menu and select Toolbar):

> Track Time Elapsed   Displays the track number and play time elapsed.
>
> Track Time Remaining   Displays the track number and time remaining for that track.
>
> Disc Time Remaining   Displays the time remaining on the disc.
>
> Random Track Order   Plays the tracks in random order.
>
> Continuous Play   After the last track has played, play continues with the first track.
>
> Intro Play   Plays only the first few seconds of each track. This helps you find the track you want to play.

 Total Control   If you want to control the order in which tracks are played, create a play list by clicking the Edit Play List button and entering the information for each track.

4. When you're through listening to your CD, click Stop if needed to stop the playback. Then click Eject to eject the CD, or press the Eject button on the drive itself.

Using Media Player

With Media Player, you can play various types of multimedia (sound and video) files, including these formats: .WAV (sound), .MID (sound), .RMI (sound), .AVI (video), and .MPEG (video).

To use Media Player, follow these steps:

1. Click the Start button, and then select Programs |
    Accessories | Entertainment | Media Player. The Media
    Player window opens, as shown in Figure 19.2.

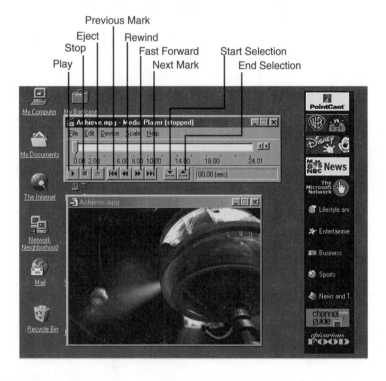

FIGURE 19.2 Media Player plays both sound and video files.

2. Open the Device menu and select the device you want to
    use. The Open dialog box appears.

3. Change to the drive and folder that contain the file you
    want to play, choose it from those listed, and click OK.

4. Click the Play button. There are other buttons you can
    click as well:

Stop   Stops the playback.

Eject   Ejects a CD-ROM from its drive.

Previous Mark and Next Mark   Rewinds or fast forwards to the beginning or the end of the file, or to the nearest selection mark.

Rewind and Fast Forward   Rewinds or fast forwards one increment at a time.

Start Selection and End Selection   Use these buttons to mark a segment of the file to play. Move the slider into position and then click either one of these buttons to mark it.

 Quick Slide   To quickly fast forward or rewind, drag the slider forward or backward to the desired position in the file.

5. When you're through listening to or viewing your file, click the × button to exit Media Player.

USING THE ACTIVEMOVIE CONTROL

The ActiveMovie Control is usually used as a helper application for your Web browser, allowing it to play any ActiveMovie files you encounter on the Web. It is also used in conjunction with Explorer and My Computer and any other application that supports embedded video objects. The control itself is very simple, so you might prefer to use Media Player to play your ActiveMovie files instead (see the preceding section for help).

USING SOUND RECORDER

With Sound Recorder, you can play sound files (.WAV). You can also record your own sounds using a simple microphone attached to your sound card. You can even add special effects to sound files!

To play a sound file, follow these steps:

1. Click Start and then select Programs | Accessories | Entertainment | Sound Recorder. Sound Recorder opens, as shown in Figure 19.3.

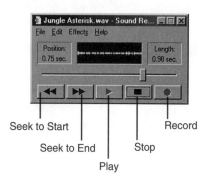

Figure 19.3   Sound Recorder plays .WAV files.

2. Open the File menu and select Open. The Open dialog box appears.

3. Change to the drive and folder that contain the sound file you want to play. Select it from those listed, and click Open.

4. Click Play. To stop the playback, click Stop. You can drag the slider to rewind or fast forward as needed.

To record a sound file with Sound Recorder, follow these steps:

1. Open the File menu and select New.

2. Click Record and begin speaking into your microphone.

3. When you're through, click Stop.

4. To review what you've recorded, click Play. When you're satisfied, open the File menu and select Save to save the recording to a file. The Save As dialog box appears.

5. Change to the drive and folder in which you want to save your file. Type a name for the sound file in the File name text box, and click Save.

Special Effects You can add an effect to your sound recording by opening the Effects menu and selecting an effect from those listed, such as Increase Speed.

Using the Volume Control

The Volume Control gives you power over Windows sound. With it, you can control the balance between your left and right speakers, adjust the volume, and even mute particular devices.

To use the Volume Control, follow these steps:

1. Double-click the speaker icon on the taskbar. The Volume Control appears, as shown in Figure 19.4.

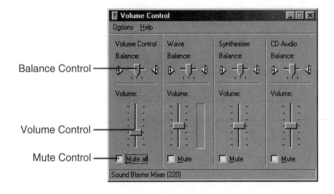

Figure 19.4 Control Windows sound with the Volume Control.

2. Initially, the controls for playback devices are displayed. To display the controls for a recording device, open the File menu and select Properties | Recording. Make sure the device you want to control is selected, and then click OK.

3. To adjust the balance between the left and right speakers, drag the Balance Control for that device to the left or right as needed.

4. To adjust the volume for a device, drag the Volume Control for that device up or down.

5. To mute a device, click its Mute option.

6. When you're through, click the × button to exit the Volume Control.

 Fast Volume   To quickly adjust the overall volume in Windows, click the speaker icon on the taskbar. A volume control appears. Drag the slider up or down to adjust the volume. A beep sounds so that you can judge the volume you selected.

In this lesson, you learned how to use each of Windows multimedia accessories. In the next lesson, you'll learn how to use the other Windows accessories.

USING OTHER ACCESSORIES

In this lesson, you'll learn how to use other Windows accessories.

USING THE CALCULATOR

Windows 98 comes with a handy calculator you can use to calculate anything you need, from balancing your checkbook to adding up the latest sales figures (see Figure 20.1). You'll find the Calculator on the Accessories menu. Using the Calculator is remarkably similar to using a regular pocket calculator: Use the + button to add, the – to subtract, / to divide, and * to multiply. To clear the last entry, click CE or press the Delete key. To clear a calculation completely, click C or press the Esc key. To compute the final value, click = or press the Enter key.

FIGURE 20.1 You can perform simple and complex calculations with the Calculator.

You can store the result of a calculation (or any number) and recall it when needed. To store the displayed value, click MS. To recall it, click MR. To add the displayed value to the value stored in memory, click M+. To clear the memory, click MC.

Mad Science? You can perform scientific calculations with the Calculator. Open the View menu and select Scientific.

Using Imaging

With Imaging, you can view your graphic images. You can zoom, rotate, and print the previewed image. You can also view a fax image.

To preview an image, follow these steps:

1. Click Start, and then select Programs | Accessories | Imaging.

2. Click the Open button on the toolbr.

3. Select the image you want to view, and then click Open. The image appears in the Imaging window.

4. Here are some of the more useful toolbar buttons and their purposes (see Figure 20.2):

Open　Opens an image for previewing.

Print　Prints the displayed image.

Zoom In　Zooms in on the displayed image.

Zoom Out　Zooms out on the displayed image.

Best Fit　Zooms the image to fit the window.

Fit to Width　Zooms the image to fit the width of the window.

Drag　Lets you move the image within the window by dragging.

Select Image　Lets you select an area of the image.

Annotation Selection　Selects an annotation for copying, moving, deleting, and so on.

Annotation Toolbar   Displays/hides the Annotation toolbar.

Rotate Left   Rotates the image to the left.

Rotate Right   Rotates the image to the right.

One-Page View   Displays one page of the document.

Thumbnail View   Shows multiple pages of the document at once, in small thumbnail-sized windows.

Page and Thumbnail View   Combines the One-Page and Thumbnail views.

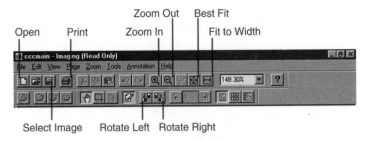

FIGURE 20.2   You can view graphic images with Imaging Preview.

USING PHONE DIALER

With Phone Dialer, you can place phone calls using your computer and its modem. This saves you the trouble of having to look up a number and then dial it. When needed, Phone Dialer can even dial your long-distance access code or calling card number. It also tracks your calls in a convenient log that you can review when needed.

To use Phone Dialer, follow these steps:

1. Click Start, and then select Programs|Accessories|
   Communications|Phone Dialer. Phone Dialer appears, as
   shown in Figure 20.3.

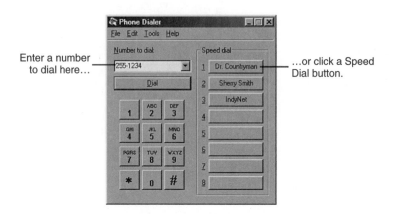

Enter a number
to dial here...

...or click a Speed
Dial button.

FIGURE 20.3   Let Phone Dialer dial frequently used numbers
for you.

2. Type the number you want to dial into the Number to
   dial text box, or click a Speed dial button.

 Speed Dial   To add a phone number to a Speed Dial
button, click an available button, type the name and phone
number of the person you're entering, and click Save.

3. Click Dial.

Phone Dialer logs each call, along with the call's duration. To
view the log, open the Tools menu and select Show Log.

In this lesson, you learned how to use the Calculator, Imaging,
and Phone Dialer accessories. In the next lesson, you'll learn how
to run your DOS applications in Windows.

RUNNING DOS APPLICATIONS

In this lesson, you'll learn how to use your DOS applications in Windows 98.

STARTING A DOS APPLICATION

When you run a DOS program under Windows 98, a private space in memory is set up just for that program. The DOS program is then given whatever system resources it needs. This protection lets the DOS program run cleanly, without compromising the needs of some other program that might be running.

DOS Application   A program that was originally designated to run on DOS (an acronym for Disk Operating System). DOS is a type of PC operating system that predates Windows operating systems. Unlike Windows, DOS does not have a graphical user interface (GUI). In DOS, you issue commands to the operating system by typing them in with your keyboard, rather than clicking graphical elements using a mouse. You can still run DOS applications on your Windows operating system, but you may need to follow special procedures described in this lesson.

You can run your DOS program in a window, making it easy to switch between it and another program, or you can run it full screen.

Not Full Screen   You can maximize a DOS window, but it might not fill the screen. Instead, depending on the program's video resolution, it might fill only part of the screen. To switch to full-screen mode, press Alt+Enter. To switch back to windowed mode, press Alt+Enter again.

There are many ways in which you can start your DOS program:

- If there's a command for the DOS program on your Start menu, click the Start button, select Programs, and then select the command to start the DOS program. (If you'd like to add a command for the program to the Start menu, see Lesson 9, "Customizing Other Attributes of Windows 98," for help.)

- If an icon for the program exists on your Desktop, click (or double-click) the icon.

- Open Windows Explorer or My Computer and click (or double-click) the program's startup file.

- Click the Start button, select Run, and then type the command to start the DOS program. Click OK.

It Won't Run!   If you have problems running your DOS program in a window, you might want to restart your PC and run it from the DOS prompt. Click Start and select Shut Down. Then select Restart in MS-DOS mode. At the DOS prompt, type the command to start the program, and press Enter. Some games need to be started this way.

CONFIGURING A DOS APPLICATION

When a DOS program is started, a special area in memory is carved out, and a certain amount of system resources is allocated to the program. Some programs might need to make some adjustments to the resource allotment in order to run properly under Windows.

Each DOS program has its own properties, just like any Windows program. To change these properties, you use the Properties dialog box:

1. Click the Properties button on the toolbar.

2. Click the appropriate tab and select the options you want. For example, to change the program's memory requirements, click the Memory tab.

3. Click OK.

Long Filenames and DOS Applications

DOS applications don't understand the longer filenames commonly used under Windows. So when saving your files, you'll need to restrict yourself to using only eight characters, plus a three-character extension, like this: CARSALES.WKS.

You don't have to worry about forgetting this requirement; the program won't let you use more characters in your filenames. But if you need to export a file from some other program and then use it in your DOS program, you'll need to remember the eight plus three restriction.

Copying, Cutting, and Pasting Text

You can copy, cut, and paste text into and out of any DOS program using the Windows Clipboard, just as you might with any Windows program. The procedure is a bit different, however:

1. The DOS program must be running in a window, as shown in Figure 21.1. So if needed, press Alt+Enter to switch to windowed mode.

Mark button   Copy button   Paste button

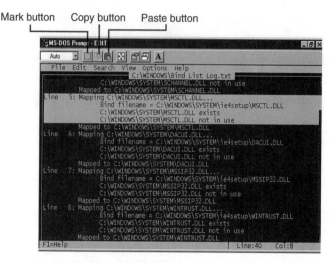

FIGURE 21.1   You can copy and cut text from a DOS application.

2. Click the Mark button on the toolbar.

3. Highlight the text you want to copy or cut.

4. To copy text, click the Copy button. The text is copied to the Clipboard. (To cut text, press the Delete key.)

5. Switch to the other program. Click where you want the text placed, and then click the Paste button you'll find on most program's toolbars. If a Paste button doesn't exist, press Ctrl+V.

In this lesson, you learned how to run your DOS programs under Windows 98. In the next lesson, you'll learn how to print your documents.

PRINTING WITH WINDOWS 98

In this lesson, you'll learn how to print your Windows documents.

INSTALLING A PRINTER

When Windows 98 was first installed on your computer, it checked for any locally attached (nonnetworked) printers and set them up automatically. However, if you've purchased a new printer recently, you'll need to install it before you can use it to print your Windows documents. In addition, before you use a network printer, it must be installed as well.

To install a new printer, follow these steps:

1. Click Start, select Settings, and select Printers. The Printers folder window appears.

2. Click (or double-click) the Add Printer icon.

3. The Add Printer Wizard appears. Click Next >.

4. Select either Local printer or Network printer. Click Next >.

5. Select the manufacturer of your printer from the Manufacturers list. Then select your printer from the Printers list. If a disk came with your new printer, click Have Disk, select the file, and click OK. Click Next >.

6. Select the port you want to use and click Next >.

7. Enter a name for your printer, and select whether you want this printer to act as the default printer for your system. Then click Next >.

8. Select Yes to print a test page, and then click Finish. You might be asked to insert your Windows disks or CD-ROM; do so if prompted. The icon for your new printer appears in the Printers folder.

Setting a Default Printer

If you use more than one printer—for example, a local printer and a network printer—you can designate one of them as the default. The default printer is the printer that your applications will use to print your documents, unless you specifically select a different printer from the Print dialog box.

The first printer set up on your computer was automatically established as the default printer. You can designate a different default printer by following these steps:

1. Click Start, select Settings, and select Printers. The Printers folder window appears.

2. Right-click the icon of the printer you want to make the default. (The current default printer appears with a small checkmark next to its icon.)

3. Select Set as Default from the shortcut menu that appears.

Printing from an Application

When you initiate a print command from within an application, the document is prepared and then passed to the print queue, where it waits in line behind any other documents you have already set to print. After the document is passed to the print queue, command is then returned to you so that you can continue working either in that same application or some other program. You don't have to wait as your document is being printed; the Windows print queue handles the entire process.

To print a document from within an application, follow these steps:

1. Open the program's File menu and select Print. A Print
   dialog box similar to the one shown in Figure 22.1 appears. You can also click the Print button on the toolbar
   (if present), but the Print dialog box won't appear and the
   default printer will be used.

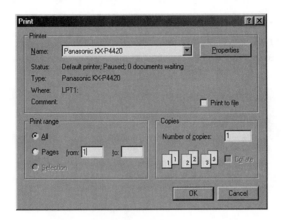

FIGURE 22.1   A typical Print dialog box.

2. The Print dialog box within your application might be
   slightly different, but it will still contain certain elements:

   From the list of printers, select the printer you want to
   use.

   Select the pages you want to print.

   If the option is available, select the number of copies
   you want to print.

3. After selecting your options, click OK.

Is What You See What You'll Get?   If you'd like to preview your print job before you actually print it, most applications offer a Print Preview option on the File menu.

CONTROLLING THE PRINT JOB

When you send a document to the printer for printing, it's placed behind any other documents that are already waiting to be printed. You can reassign the order of printing, cancel a print job, or pause the printer while you change the paper.

When you view the print queue, as shown in Figure 22.2, each document is listed, along with its print status, owner, number of pages, and the time and date that printing was initiated.

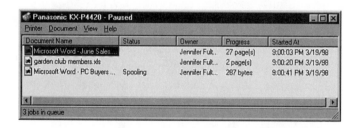

FIGURE 22.2   Documents waiting to be printed appear in the print queue.

To display the print queue, do either of the following:

- Double-click the Printer icon on the taskbar.

- In the Printers folder, double-click the icon for the printer whose queue you want to check.

REORDERING THE JOBS IN THE QUEUE

To reorder a document within the queue, click it and drag it in the list wherever you want. However, you can't place a document in front of a document that is *currently printing*.

PAUSING AND RESUMING THE QUEUE

You can pause the print queue at any time. This might be necessary if the printer is jammed or some other problem has developed. By pausing the print queue, you can easily correct the problem and then resume printing when you're ready.

To pause the printing, follow these steps:

1. Double-click the Printer icon on the taskbar to open the print queue.

2. Open the Printer menu and select Pause Printing. A check mark appears next to this command.

To resume printing, open the Printer menu and select Pause Printing again to remove the check mark.

 Printer Stalled   If your printer runs out of paper, Windows will automatically pause the printing process and display a message telling you what's happened. If you don't respond, Windows will automatically retry the printer in five seconds.

DELETING A PRINT JOB

If you notice that you've sent the wrong document to the printer, or that you need to make some small change, it's not too late. You can delete a print job from the queue to prevent it from being printed. Follow these steps:

1. Double-click the Printer icon on the taskbar to open the print queue.

2. Select the document you want to delete from the queue.

3. Open the Document menu and select Cancel Printing, or press the Delete key.

To remove *all* documents from the print queue, open the Printer menu and select Purge Print Documents.

In this lesson, you learned how print your Windows documents. In the next lesson, you'll learn how to keep your hard disk in shape.

23 DISK MANAGEMENT

In this lesson, you'll learn how to perform routine maintenance on your hard disk.

BACKING UP YOUR HARD DISK

To protect your valuable data, it's best to make an extra copy of it. The easiest way to do so is to back up your files onto disk or tape. Then, if something happens to the original file, you can restore the backup copy onto your hard disk.

When you perform a backup, it's not necessary to back up every file on your hard disk. You should back up your document files and certain system files, but you don't need to back up program files, because they can be reinstalled if needed from their original installation disks.

PERFORMING A BACKUP

To back up some or all of the files on your hard disk, follow these steps:

1. Click Start, and then select Programs | Accessories | System Tools | Backup.

2. The first time you start Microsoft Backup, it checks to see if you have any backup devices (such as a tape drive) on your computer. If you do have a backup device, click Yes, and follow the steps in the Add Hardware Wizard to install it. If not, click No. (If you've used Microsoft Backup before, skip to step 3.)

3. A welcome screen appears, as shown in Figure 23.1. Select Create a new backup job and click OK.

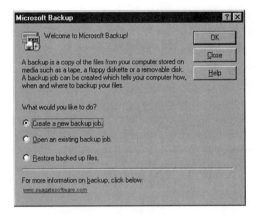

FIGURE 23.1   Welcome to Microsoft Backup.

 What Happens Next Time?   After you create a backup job, you can use it to back up the same files later. When you select Open an existing backup job at the welcome screen shown in Figure 23.1, you're taken to an Open Backup Job dialog box where you can select the job to open. After you select the job, you're taken to the main Backup screen, where you can begin the backup job by pressing Start. You can also change the parameters of the original job if needed.

4. Select Back up My Computer or Back up selected files, folders, and drives. Click Next >. If you selected Back up My Computer, skip to step 6.

5. You're taken to the Backup Wizard, where you select the items you want backed up (selected files appear with a check mark, as shown in Figure 23.2), and then click Next >:

> To back up all the files on a drive, click next to a drive letter.
>
> To back up all the files in a folder, click next to a folder. (To display folders on a drive, click the drive.)

To select only some files in a folder, click the folder's plus sign to display its subfolders. Then click the subfolder that contains the files you want to back up to display its files in the panel on the right. Click the files you want to select.

To deselect a particular file, click it again to remove the check mark.

After you select the folders or files, click Next > to return to the Backup Wizard.

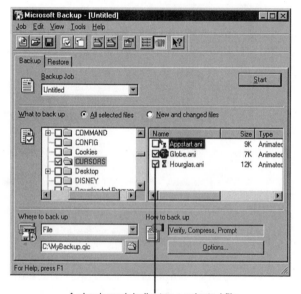

A check mark indicates a selected file

FIGURE 23.2   Select the files you want to back up.

6. Select All selected files or New and changed files. Click Next >, which takes you to the Backup Wizard. If you select New and changed files, files are backed up only if they've changed since the last backup you performed. If you select this option, *do not use the same backup disks you used before.* Use a new set of disks.

7. By default, backups are stored in the root directory of drive C:. To select another drive or folder, click the folder

icon on the Backup Wizard. Select the drive and folder on which you want your backup stored from the Where to backup screen of the Backup Wizard. Click Next >.

8. Select the options you want, and then click Next >. You're taken to the How to backup screen of the Backup Wizard, and you're asked to select preferences from the following:

   Compare original and backup files to verify data was successfully backed up   This option makes the backup process longer, but it does guarantee that all files are backed up successfully.

   Compress the backup data to save space   This option compresses (shrinks) your files so that they take up less space on disk. Click Next >.

9. Type a name for this backup job, such as Full Backup. You can later reuse this job to complete the same type of backup procedure. This screen also summarizes this backup job with a what, where, how, and when description. Click Start.

10. While Backup is in progress, you have the option of canceling the backup. When the backup is complete, you'll see a message telling you so. Click OK.

11. Click Report on the Backup Progress dialog box to review the backup summary. Close the report window after you review it and click OK in the Backup Progress dialog box when you're through.

12. The main Microsoft Backup window appears. Click its Close button in the upper-right corner to exit.

RESTORING FILES

If a file is accidentally deleted or damaged in some way, you can restore it from your most recent backup. Follow these steps:

1. Click Start, and then select Programs | Accessories | System Tools | Backup.

2. Select Restore backed up files. Click OK >.

3. You're taken to the Restore Wizard. Choose where to restore files from. Click the folder iconto select the drive and folder in which your backup is stored. Click Next >.

4. Select the backup set that contains the files you want to restore. Click OK.

5. Select the files you want to restore from the following list(selected files appear with a check mark) and click Next >:

> To restore all the backed-up files on a drive, click next to a drive letter.

> To restore all the backed-up files in a folder, click next to a folder.

> To restore only some of the backed-up files in a folder, click the folder's plus sign to display its subfolders. Then click the folder that contains the documents you want to restore to display its files in the panel on the right. Click the files you want to select.

> To deselect a particular file, click it again, and the check mark is removed.

6. Select whether you want files restored to their Original Location or an Alternate Location (another drive or folder). If you select Alternate Location, click the folder icon and select the drive and folder you want to use. After selecting where to restore, click OK within that Browse for folder box. Click Next >.

7. Select the replacement option you want to use:

> Do not replace the file on my computer   Use this option if you want to restore only files that no longer exist on your hard disk.

> Replace the file on my computer only if the file is older   This will restore all files, provided that they are *newer* than the files already on the hard disk.

Always replace the file on my computer   This option restores all the files on the backup, even if some of those files are older than the ones already on your hard disk.

8. Click Start.

9. You'll see a Media Required message telling you what media are required to complete the operation. Click OK.

10. When the restoration is complete, you'll see a message telling you so. Click OK.

11. Click Report on the Restore Progress dialog box to review the restoration summary. Close the report box after you review it. Click OK on the Restore Progress dialog box when you're through.

12. The main Microsoft Backup window appears. Click its Close button in the upper-right corner to exit.

DEFRAGMENTING YOUR DISK

When a file is stored to a disk, it's broken into chunks, and each piece is stored in the first available sector. After the disk starts getting full, and files are deleted (making certain sectors available), file parts are no longer saved in adjacent sectors.

Thus, a file may be scattered (or *fragmented*) over the disk, which can slow down its retrieval of files. To improve the speed of your PC, you should *defragment* your hard disk. Defragmenting reorganizes the parts of each file so that they are once again adjacent to each other on the hard disk, eliminating excess search time.

To defragment your hard disk, follow these steps:

1. Click Start, and then select Programs | Accessories | System Tools | Disk Defragmenter. The Disk Defragmenter Wizard appears.

2. Select the drive you want to defragment (see Figure 23.3). Select particular settings by clicking the Settings button. You can choose whether to rearrange program files so

programs start faster and to check the drive for errors. Also, you can use these options this time only or each time you defragment. Click OK after selecting options to close the Settings dialog box.

3. Click OK, and the defragmentation process begins. You can view a graphical representation of the process by pressing Show Details.

Figure 23.3   Select the drive to defragment.

4. It is normally recommended that you not use the computer during defragmentation. If you use the computer during defragmentation, you may preventoptimal results. To stop the defragmentation process temporarily, click Pause. To stop it completely, click Stop.

5. When the process is complete, you'll see a message telling you so and asking if you want to quit Disk Defragmenter. Click OK.

Scanning Your Disk

Sometimes a file isn't stored to disk properly, and the computer loses part of it. This sometimes happens when a file is deleted, and the references to all the parts of the file aren't removed from the main file directory (File Allocation Table). In any case, it's a good idea to periodically check your hard disk for this type of error, and to let the computer fix the problems it finds.

To scan your hard disk for errors, follow these steps:

1. Click Start, and then select Programs | Accessories | System Tools | ScanDisk.

2. Select the drive you want to scan.

3. Select the type of scanning you want to perform. Standard checks the hard disk for file errors. Thorough checks for errors and examines the surface of the hard disk.

4. If you want ScanDisk to fix any errors it finds (rather than reporting those errors to you and providing various options), select the Automatically fix errors option. To select some advanced options, press Advanced and make your selections. Then click OK.

5. When you're ready, click Start.

6. When the scanning is through, you'll see a message showing the ScanDisk Results. Click Close.

7. You're returned to the ScanDisk dialog box. Click Close.

SCHEDULING TASKS

With Windows Maintenance Wizard, you can schedule regular maintenance tasks to be performed on your computer's hard disk. These tasks include the following:

- Scheduling programs to open when you start your PC

- Defragmenting the hard disk

- Checking the disk for errors using ScanDisk

- Deleting unneeded files

To schedule tasks, follow these steps:

1. Click Start, and then select Programs | Accessories | System Tools | Maintenance Wizard.

2. Select Express or Custom, and click Next >.

3. Select a time period when you want to have maintenance done, and click Next >. If you selected Express in step 2, skip to step 8. If you selected Custom, continue to step 4.

4. A listing of the programs that are currently scheduled to be run at start-up appears. To prevent a program from running at start-up, click it to remove the check mark. Click Next >.

5. To schedule Disk Defragmenter to run automatically, click Yes, defragment my disk regularly. If you want to change the time at which this occurs, click Reschedule. Make your selections. Then click OK. To change the drive to defragment, click Settings and make your selections. Then click OK.When you're ready, click Next >.

6. To schedule ScanDisk to run automatically, click Yes, scan my hard disk for errors regularly. If you want to change the time at which this occurs, click Reschedule. Make your selections. Then click OK. To change the drive that you want scanned (among other options), click Settings. Make your selections. Then click OK. When you're done, click Next >.

7. To have Windows delete unneeded files, click Yes, delete unnecessary files regularly. To change the time at which this occurs, click Reschedule. Make your selections. Then click OK. To change the types of files that are automatically deleted, click Settings. Make your selections. Then click OK. When you're done, click Next >.

8. A summary screen appears. Review the tasks that have been scheduled. If youwant to change the tasks, you can click < Back to return to a previous screen and change your selections. If everything's okay, click Finish. (If you want the tasks you selected to be performed *now*, select When I click Finish, perform each scheduled task for the first time.)

9. You may see a dialog box asking if you want to convert your drives to a more efficient format called FAT32. If you do, click Yes.

CHECKING YOUR SYSTEM FOR PROBLEMS

If you ever run into trouble with your computer, you can use the System Information tool to help you diagnose the problem and fix it. For example, if you contact a technical support person about a problem with your monitor, System Information can provide detailed configuration information about its setup. In addition, System Information provides many easy to use tools that you can use to fix particular problems yourself.

To start System Information and display configuration information:

1. Click Start, select Programs, select Accessories, select System Tools, then select System Information.

2. If you're having a problem with a particular piece of hardware, check out the computer resources it's using. To view hardware resources such as DMA, IRQ, and I/O addresses, click the plus sign in front of Hardware Resources, then click on the appropriate category, such as DMA. Or, to instead see a list of hardware or drivers that might be sharing the same resources (and therefore, in conflict with each other), click Conflicts/Sharing.

3. To view detailed information about a particular peripheral, click the plus sign in front of Components, then click the hardware you wish to view, such as Display.

4. If you're having problems with a particular program, the information displayed under Software Environment might help your technical support person discover the source of the problem.

Use the utilities on System Information's Tools menu to troubleshoot and repair various system problems:

- Update Wizard Uninstall   Use this tool to remove Windows 98 updates you may have installed.

- Signature Verification Tool   This tool uses digital signatures—very, very long series of digits attached by software manufacturers to their files—to authenticate that these files did indeed originate from the source whose signature appears in the file. As signatures become more prevalent, this tool will gain wider use in Windows 98.

- Windows Report Tool   Use this tool to prepare a report about your system problem for the Microsoft Technical Support staff.

- System File Checker   Checks your Windows system files for errors.

- Registry Checker   Checks the Windows' System Registry for errors.

- Automatic Skip Driver Agent   Allows you to control a feature of Windows 98 that identifies which driver (if any) is responsible for a failed startup sequence, and avoids loading that driver automatically next time around.

- Dr. Watson   Loads Dr. Watson, a program that monitors system activity. With Dr. Watson loaded, you'll see a doctor with a stethoscope in the lower right corner of the taskbar. If your computer locks up, Dr. Watson's log—a text file that was being compiled before the lockup occured—can help you discover what program may be causing the problem.

- System Configuration Utility   Graphically displays the contents of critical files such as CONFIG.SYS, AUTOEXEC.BAT, WIN.INI, and SYSTEM.INI, plus those tools and external programs that Windows loads auto-matically upon startup, so that you can turn features and settings on or off without opening up Notepad and mak-ing those changes by hand.

- ScanDisk   A back door (or alternate route), if you will, into the ScanDisk program, which checks for errors on your hard disk drives.

- Version Conflict Manager   Allows you to restore an older version of a Windows system file.

In this lesson, you learned how to perform basic maintenance tasks on your hard disk. In the next lesson, you'll learn how to use Internet Explorer, a Web browser.

USING INTERNET EXPLORER

In this lesson, you'll learn how to enter addresses into Internet Explorer and how to move from page to page on the Web.

USING THE INTERNET EXPLORER BROWSER

Internet Explorer is a program you can use to view Web sites on the World Wide Web (WWW). You can access the Web through either Windows Explorer or the Internet Explorer Browser, both of which are really the same program. By starting with the Internet Explorer, you get the benefit of already being in Internet mode.

To start Internet Explorer, follow these steps:

1. Click (or double-click) the Internet Explorer icon on the Desktop.

2. If you're not currently connected to the Internet, you'll see the Dial-up Connection screen, shown in Figure 24.1. Type your Password and click Connect.

 I Don't Have a Connection! If you need to establish your Internet connection, see Appendix B, "Configuring for the Internet or an Online Service," for help.

3. Internet Explorer displays your home page. From here, you can enter the address of a page you want to view, or you can search for an address. You can also click a link to display a different page. You'll learn how to enter an

address and click a link later in this lesson; you'll learn
how to search the Internet in Lesson 25, "Searching for
and Saving Web Page Locations."

Enter your
password here

Figure 24.1   Connecting to the Internet.

 Home Page   When you first start Internet Explorer, it
takes you to your *home page*. This page is typically associated with the Web browser you installed, so in this case,
you're taken to Microsoft's site on the Web. You can
change your home page to any Web page you like.

Going to a Specific Site

Every page on the Web has a specific address. To view a page, you
enter its address into Internet Explorer. A typical address looks
something like this:

http://cws.internet.com/32menu.html

Briefly, here's what each part means:

http:/	Hypertext Transfer Protocol, the language of the Web
/cws.internet.com	The address of a site on the Web
/32menu.html	The name of a Web page on the CWS site

To enter an address into Internet Explorer, do the following:

1. Type the address into the Address text box.

2. Press Enter. The page whose address you typed is displayed. (To stop a page from being displayed, click the Stop button.)

 My Page Didn't Display! Try checking what you've typed. Make sure you've used / and not \, and then press Enter again or click Refresh. If that doesn't work, delete the filename from the address, and see if you can connect to the site's home page. If everything else fails, you might have to search for the page's correct address. See Lesson 25 for help.

Following a Link

One way to move from page to page is by clicking a *link* (short for *hyperlink*). A link is usually a bit of underlined text, typically blue in color (although it can be any color), as shown in Figure 24.2.

A link may also be a graphic image. When you move the mouse over a link, whether it's a bit of text or a graphic, the mouse cursor changes to a hand. The address of the link's associated page appears in the Status bar at the bottom of the screen.

To use a link, just click it. When you do, you're automatically taken to the Web page that the link refers to. If you later return to the page that contained the link, you'll notice that the link you clicked has changed color, typically from blue to purple (although, again, it could be any color). This change lets you quickly identify the links you've visited.

When you pass the
cursor over a link, it
changes to a hand.   A graphic link.

The address to which the link   A text link.
refers appears in the Status bar.

FIGURE 24.2   A link may be text or a graphic.

RETURNING TO A PREVIOUSLY VIEWED PAGE

As you move from page to page, a history of the pages you've
visited is kept. This makes it easy to retrace your steps as needed.
Table 24.1 explains some of your options.

TABLE 24.1   NAVIGATION BUTTONS

ACTION	BUTTON TO CLICK
Move back in the history	Back
Move forward again	Forward
Return to the Home page	Home
View cool Web pages	Best of the Web
View hot new Web pages	Today's Link

 Complete History   You can move back and forth through the history several pages at a time by clicking the down arrow on the Back and Forward buttons.

USING HISTORY

You can also return to a previously viewed page by selecting it from the History list. To display this list, click the History button on the Standard Buttons toolbar. This list appears on the left side of the Internet Explorer window. Initially, pages you've viewed today are displayed. To display the pages from a different day, click that day in the list. To revisit a particular site, click it.

In this lesson, you learned how to use Internet Explorer to explore the Web. In the next lesson, you'll learn how to search for particular Web pages.

25 SEARCHING FOR AND SAVING WEB PAGE LOCATIONS

In this lesson, you'll learn how to locate specific Web pages and save their locations for future use.

UNDERSTANDING SEARCHES

Search engines are free tools that let you sort through the vast amount of information available on the Internet. If you don't have much luck with one search engine, you can always try another, because each one maintains its own list of pages, and each one indexes those pages differently.

Some search engines let you browse their index by selecting a series of categories and subcategories until you find the desired Web site. Other search engines let you search for a page using a *form*. You enter the criteria you want to search for into the form, and then a list of pages that match that criteria appears. Then you simply click a link to one of the listed pages.

 Form A form looks similar to a dialog box. Like a dialog box, you enter the requested information into the form, click a button such as Search or Submit, and the information in the form is processed.

Here are some tips to remember when entering search criteria:

- Try to be as specific as possible. For example, you'll have better luck searching for Michigan bass fishing than just fishing.

- Do not include common words such as "to", "the", "an", "who", and so on. The search engine will just ignore them.

- The word "and" is understood. For example, if you type **cigarette tax**, the search engine will look for pages that contain both the word cigarette *and* the word tax, although not necessarily in that order, or even together.

- To search for two or more words together, enclose them in quotations, as in **"cigarette tax"**.

- You can use the word "or" when needed. For example, you might search for **Indiana OR Ohio**.

- You can combine phrases, as in Indiana OR Ohio **"cigarette tax"**.

- To make sure that a certain word is not included in the search results, use the NOT operator, as in **Indian NOT American**, which will get you documents on people from India, not American Indians.

- Some search engines let you use wildcards. For example, if you type **stock***, you'll get matches for stockbroker, stockyard, stock exchange, and stocks.

- Some search engines let you use parentheses to create more complex search criteria: **("infant car seat" OR "baby seat") AND safety**.

- Some search engines let you enter "search busters," which are words that either must (or must not) be found within a page in order for that page to be included in the search results. A plus or a minus sign is used to indicate a search buster, as in **+civil**.

Table 25.1 lists search operators (such as AND and OR) for the most popular search engines. N/A indicates that a particular option isn't supported by that search engine.

TABLE 25.1 SEARCH OPERATORS YOU CAN USE

OPERATOR	ALTAVISTA	EXCITE	LYCOS	INFOSEEK	YAHOO!
And	AND, &	AND	assumed	+	N/A
Or	OR,		OR	N/A	–	N/A
Not	NOT	NOT	–	N/A	N/A
Quotes	" "	" "	N/A	" "	" "
Rule	( )	( )	N/A	N/A	N/A
Wildcard	*	N/A	$	N/A	N/A
Must include	+	+	N/A	N/A	+
Must not include	–	–	–	N/A	–

USING SEARCH ENGINES

Here are some of the most popular search engines:

AltaVista **http://altavista.digital.com**

Excite **http://www.excite.com**

Lycos **http://www.lycos.com**

InfoSeek **http://www.infoseek.com**

Yahoo! **http://www.yahoo.com**

Internet Explorer provides quick access to these and many other search engines. To use a search engine to locate a Web page, follow these steps:

1. In Internet Explorer, click Search.

2. The search page for the search engine being featured today appears in the left panel, as shown in Figure 25.1.

3. Select the search engine you want to use by clicking the Choose a Search Engine link, and selecting the search engine from the page that appears in the right panel (see Figure 25.1). (To redisplay this page later on, select List all Search Engines from the Choose a Search Engine list.)

Type your search criteria here

Select the search engine you want to use

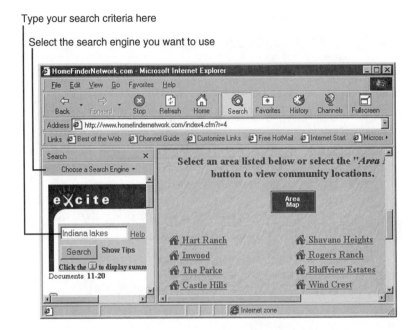

FIGURE 25.1   Searching the Web.

4. Type your search criteria in the text box.

5. Click Search. You may see a warning telling you that you're about to send the information included in the form over the Internet. Since you didn't type any private information into the form, click Yes to continue.

6. After a list of matching pages is returned, scroll down the list until you find a page you like, and click its link. The page appears in the panel on the right, as shown in Figure 25.2.

How Likely Is It?   Sometimes a percentage appears in front of each listing that tells you the likelihood that a particular page fits your search criteria.

Click a link to a page you like   The page appears here

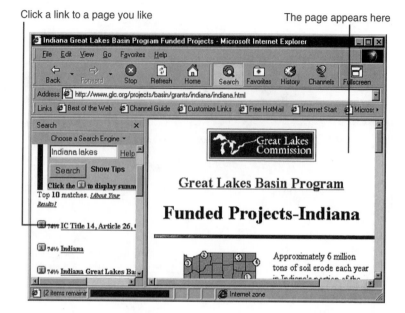

FIGURE 25.2   Your search results.

7. To remove the Search panel, click its × button.

 Quick Search   You can also start the search by typing either **go**, **find**, or **?** in the Address text box, followed by your search criteria, as in **find Indiana lakes**. Internet Explorer initiates the search using the current search engine.

You can also initiate a search by clicking Start and then selecting Find | On the Internet.

SEARCHING A WEB PAGE

You can search the text within a Web page just as you might search for text within a word processing document. Follow these steps:

1. In Internet Explorer, open the Edit menu and select Find (on this page).

2. Type what you want to search for in the Find what text box.

3. Select any options you want:

   Match whole word only   Won't search for words that contain the word you typed. For example, if you type for, it won't match the word forward.

   Match case   Will search only for words that match exactly what you typed. For example, if you type Windows, it won't match the word windows.

4. Initially, Find searches the page from the top down. To search in the other direction, select Up.

5. Click Find Next. If a match is found, it's highlighted in the page. To continue the search, click Find Next again. When you're through searching, click Cancel.

Searching for People

Do you want to locate a long-lost friend or acquaintance? Maybe Internet Explorer can help, by connecting you with the most popular people-search engines on the Internet.

To search for someone, follow these steps:

1. Click Start, and then select Find | People.

2. Select the search engine you want to use from the Look in list. (You can also search for a name within your own address book.)

3. Type the Name or the E-mail address of the person you're looking for.

4. Click Find Now. A list of people matching your criteria appears.

USING THE FAVORITES FOLDER

Once you find a page on the Internet that you like, you can save it in the Favorites folder. That way, if you want to revisit the page later, you can do so without having to enter its address.

When you add a page to the Favorites folder, you can subscribe to it at the same time. By subscribing, you can have Internet Explorer notify you when the contents of the page has changed. You can also instruct Internet Explorer to download the page for you so that you can read its new contents off-line (disconnected from the Internet).

ADDING FAVORITES

To add a page to the Favorites folder, follow these steps:

1. Jump to the page you want to add to the Favorites folder.

2. Open the Favorites menu and select Add to Favorites. The Add Favorite dialog box, shown in Figure 25.3, appears.

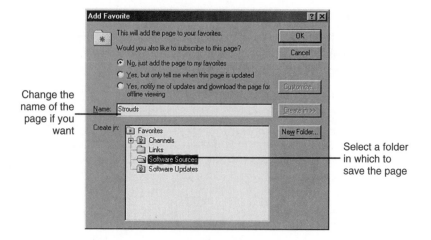

FIGURE 25.3   Save pages you like to the Favorites folder.

3. Select whether you want to subscribe to this page.

4. If you like, type a new name for the page.

5. You can organize your saved pages in subfolders in order to make it easier to locate them later. For example, you might want to create a folder called News, and save your favorite news sources in that folder. To place the page in a subfolder, click on and go to the Create in box. Otherwise, skip to step 7.

6. Select the subfolder to which you want to add the page. To create a new subfolder, click New Folder, type the name of the subfolder you want to create, and click OK.

7. Click OK to add the page to your Favorites.

To visit the page later, click the Favorites button on the Standard Buttons toolbar. Then click the page you want to visit. If you've placed the page in a subfolder, click the subfolder to reveal its contents, and then click the page you want to view.

ADDING A FAVORITE TO THE LINKS BAR

If you find a page you think you'll visit often, you can add it to the Links bar, located just under the Address bar. Pages that are added to the Links bar appear as buttons. To visit one of the pages, click its button.

To add a page to the Links bar, do any of the following:

- Drag the icon that appears next to the page's address in the Address text box onto the Links bar.

- Drag a link that appears on a Web page onto the Links bar.

- If the page has already been added to your Favorites folder, click the Favorites button on the Standard Buttons toolbar to display the Favorites list. Drag the page from its location in the list to the Links folder.

In this lesson, you learned how to locate a particular Web page and how to save its location for future use. In the next lesson, you'll learn how to send and receive electronic mail.

26 SENDING AND RECEIVING MAIL WITH OUTLOOK EXPRESS

In this lesson, you'll learn how to send and receive electronic mail messages using Outlook Express.

Windows 98 provides two programs you can use to send and receive electronic mail—Windows Messaging and Outlook Express. Outlook Express is richer in features and more closely intertwined with the Internet Explorer browser. However, most of the details in this lesson apply to Windows Messaging as well.

SENDING A MESSAGE

You can send simple text messages. You can even attach files of any type. The recipient can then detach the files and view them on his computer.

To send an email message to someone, you need his email address. An email address might look like this:

jfulton@indy.net

The first part of the address, **jfulton**, is the person's *username*—the name by which that person is known by his mail server (the computer that processes his mail). The second part of the address, **indy.net**, is the name of the mail server that handles that particular person's e-mail.

 Save That Address! Save the addresses you use most often in the Address Book for quick access.

To send an email message using Outlook Express, follow these steps:

1. Start Outlook Express by clicking (or double-clicking) the Outlook Express icon on the desktop. From within Internet Explorer, click the Mail button on the Standard Buttons toolbar and select New Message.

2. If needed, click the arrow next to the Compose Message button and select the type of stationery you want to use. If you prefer to not use stationery, select No Stationery from the menu that appears. The New Message window appears, as shown in Figure 26.1.

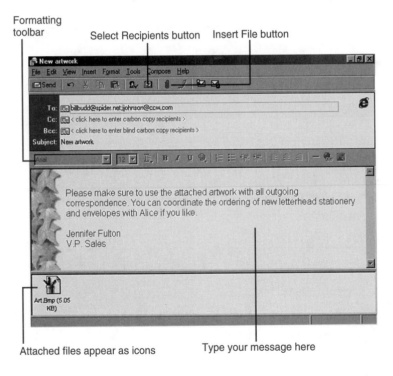

FIGURE 26.1   Creating an email message.

More Stationery! There are more patterns to choose from than those listed on the Compose Message menu. Select More Stationery from the menu, and then select the pattern you want to use from the expanded listing.

3. Click in the To: box and type the address of the person to whom you want to send your message. To add a second person, type a semicolon (;) followed by the second address. Repeat for additional people. (After you've entered addresses into your Address Book, you can click the Select Recipients button to select the address you want to use.)

Watch That Case! Be sure to use the correct case (upper and lower) when entering an e-mail address. For example, **JFulton@indy.net** is not the same as **jfulton@indy.net** or **Jfulton@Indy.net**.

4. In the Subject box, type a description of your message.

5. Click in the text area and type your message. You can use the buttons on the Formatting toolbar to enhance your text with bold, italic, color, a change in font or font size, and so on.

Who Will See It? Not everyone will see your fancy formatting—only people who use an email program such as Outlook Express that supports the use of HTML formatting. They will, however, be able to see your plain text just fine.

6. To attach a file to your message, click the Insert File button. Select the file you want to send and click Attach.

7. Make sure you're connected to the Internet, and then click Send to send the message.

Check That Message!   You can spell check your messages before you send them. Open the Tools menu and select Spelling. You can even set up Outlook Express so that it always spell checks your mail automatically. Open the Tools menu of the main Outlook Exress window and select Options. Click the Spelling tab and select the Always check spelling before sending option.

Wrong Address!   If for some reason your message couldn't be delivered, you'll be notified via email.

Using the Windows Address Book

You should save the addresses you use often in the Address Book so that you don't have to type them in each time you want to use them. To enter someone into the Address Book, follow the next steps.

Importing Addresses   The first time you start Outlook Express, it will ask you if you would like to import your addresses and messages from the Windows Messaging (Microsoft Exchange) program. If you've been using this program, it's a good idea to import your addresses into Outlook Express. You may or may not want to import old messages. In any case, follow the steps in the Import Wizard that appears.

1. Click the Address Book button on the Standard Buttons toolbar.

2. Click the New Contact button. The Properties dialog box appears, as shown in Figure 26.2.

Type an email address
here and click Add   Type a name here

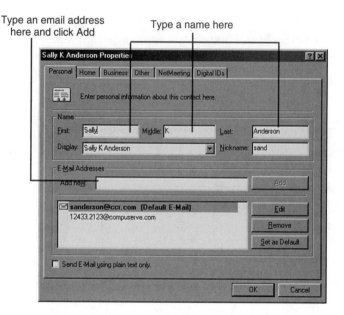

FIGURE 26.2   Adding a new contact to the Address Book.

3. Enter the contact's name in the First, Middle, and Last text boxes.

4. Type a Nickname for this contact. You can enter this nickname in the To field of a message to quickly address the message to this person.

5. Select how you want the contact to be displayed on the Display list. Typically, you'll display your contacts by name, company name, or nickname, although you can type anything you want in this field.

6. Type the contact's email address in the Add new text box and click Add. Repeat this step to add additional email addresses.

7. If you know for sure that this person uses an email program that doesn't support the use of HTML formatting, select the Send E-Mail using plain text only option.

8. This is all the information you have to enter; you can enter additional personal and business information for this contact using the other tabs if you like. When you're through, click OK.

By Group   You can place several addresses in a single group and use that group to send an email message to everyone in the group. To create a group, click the New Group button in the Address Book window. Enter a name for the group and select the addresses you want to add.

If someone sends you an email message, you can quickly add that person to the Address Book. Just open the message in a window (covered later in this lesson) and select Tools | Add to Address Book | Sender.

ADDRESSING A MESSAGE USING THE ADDRESS BOOK

To use the Address Book to address a message, follow these steps:

1. Within the Compose Message window, click the Select Recipients button on the Standard Buttons toolbar, or click the address card icon next to the To field. The Select Recipients dialog box, shown in Figure 26.3, appears.

2. Select a name or a group from the list.

3. Click the appropriate button: To, Cc, or Bcc.

4. Click OK.

Quick Addressing   If you entered a nickname for a contact when you originally created the address, type the nickname in the To, Cc, or Bcc field of the new message. Outlook Express automatically converts the nickname to a proper address.

Select a contact   Click the appropriate button

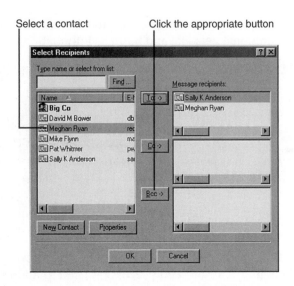

FIGURE 26.3   Select a contact for your message.

CHECKING FOR NEW MESSAGES

By default, Outlook Express automatically checks for new email messages every 30 minutes and downloads them to your system. When new mail arrives, a small beep sounds, and a new mail icon (an envelope) appears on the Status bar.

You can check for new messages whenever you like. Follow these steps:

1. Click the Send and Receive button on the Standard Buttons toolbar.

2. If prompted, enter your email password and click OK.

3. Outlook Express sends any outgoing messages and checks for new mail. Incoming mail is placed in your Inbox. To view a message, click its header in the message list, as shown in Figure 26.4. The contents of the message appear in the Preview pane.

Messages with file attachments have a paper clip icon.

When you click a message...

Unread messages appear in bold.

...its contents appear in the Preview pane.

FIGURE 26.4   Checking your messages.

If you want to open a message in its own window, double-click it. You might want to do this in order to add the sender's name to your Address Book (as explained in the preceding section) or to view a long message more clearly.

SAVING FILE ATTACHMENTS

If someone has sent you a message with a file attached to it, you will need to detach the file before you can open and use it. Follow these steps:

1. Double-click the message that contains the file attachment to open the message in its own window. Messages with file attachments have a paper clip icon next to the sender's name.

2. An icon for the attachment appears below the message text. Open the File menu and select Save Attachments.

3. Select the name of the file you want to save from the cascading menu that appears.

4. Change to the drive and folder in which you want to save the attachment, and then click Save. You can rename the file if you like by typing a new name in the File name text box.

Replying to Messages

After you've received and read a message, you can reply to it if you like. You can also forward the message to someone else if needed. Follow these steps:

1. Click the message to which you want to reply.

2. Click either Reply to Author or Reply to All (to reply to everyone who received a copy of the original message). To forward the message to someone, click Forward Message.

3. The New Message window opens. The text of the original message is automatically copied into the text area. Type your reply or comments above this text.

 Been There, Seen That You can delete all or part of the original message if you feel that the recipient doesn't need to see it again. Just select the text and press the Delete key.

4. In a reply, the message is automatically addressed to the sender (and all recipients, if you selected that option). Click Send to send the reply. If you're forwarding the message, type an address in the To box and click Send.

DELETING OLD MESSAGES

You should occasionally review your messages and delete the ones you no longer need. This reduces the amount of space your messages consume and makes Outlook Express more efficient.

To delete a message, follow these steps:

1. Select the messages you want to delete by pressing Ctrl and clicking them.

2. Press the Delete key or click the Delete button on the Standard Buttons toolbar.

3. If you use an IMAP mail server, open the File menu and select Clear Deleted Messages to remove messages from the server.

Deleted messages aren't actually deleted. Instead, they are moved to the Deleted Items folder. To empty the folder, right-click the folder name and select Empty Folder from the shortcut menu.

You can set up Outlook Express so that it always empties the Deleted Items folder when you exit the program. Just open the Tools menu and select Options. Click the General tab and select the Empty messages from the "Deleted Items" folder on exit option.

In this lesson, you learned how to send and receive electronic messages with Outlook Express. In the next lesson, you'll learn how to read and post newsgroup messages.

USING OUTLOOK EXPRESS NEWS

In this lesson, you'll learn how to read and post newsgroup messages using Outlook Express.

VIEWING AND SUBSCRIBING TO A NEWSGROUP

Newsgroups are the Internet equivalent of your company bulletin board. There are many Internet newsgroups, each focusing on a particular area of interest, from deep-sea fishing to space exploration. No matter what your hobbies or special interests are, you can probably find an Internet newsgroup that focuses on them.

SUBSCRIBING TO NEWSGROUPS

The first thing you need to do is download the list of available newsgroups from your news server. You then select the newsgroups you want to view and download the posted messages in those groups (a process called *subscribing*). Follow these steps:

1. Connect to the Internet and start Outlook Express.

2. Click the newsgroup folder.

3. You'll be asked if you would like to view a list of available newsgroups. Click Yes. The Newsgroups dialog box appears, as shown in Figure 27.1. (If the Newsgroups dialog box does not appear, click the Newsgroups button.)

4. Double-click a newsgroup to subscribe to it. To view a list of newsgroups on a particular topic, type that topic in the Display newsgroups which contain text box.

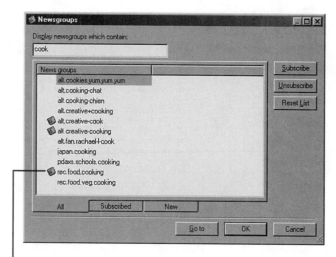

Subscribed-to newsgroups have a newspaper icon

FIGURE 27.1 Available newsgroups.

 Try Before You Buy If you want to preview a news-group before you subscribe to it, select it and click Go to.

5. When you're through selecting newsgroups to which you want to subscribe, click OK.

VIEWING MESSAGES

After subscribing to the newsgroups that interest you, you're ready to download the messages in a newsgroup so that you can view them. Follow these steps:

1. In the left panel, select the newsgroup whose messages you want to view, as shown in Figure 27.2.

2. Go to the Tools menu and select Download this Newsgroup. In the dialog that appears, check Get the following items and select New headers. Click OK.

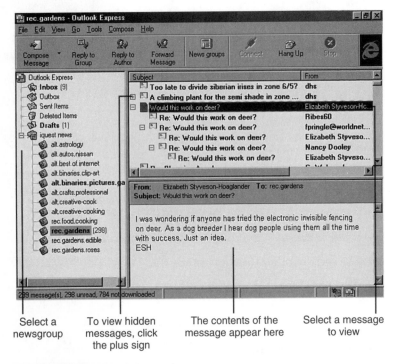

Select a   To view hidden   The contents of the   Select a message
newsgroup   messages, click   message appear here   to view
                 the plus sign

FIGURE 27.2   Viewing newsgroup messages.

Offline Viewing   If you would rather download all the
messages in the newsgroup and then disconnect from
the Internet before viewing them, you should select New
message (headers and bodies).

3. Click a message whose contents you want to view. The
headers for messages you haven't yet viewed are displayed
in bold text. After you select a message, its contents appear in the lower panel.

Quick Viewing   To view the next message, press Ctrl+>.
To view the next *unread* message, press Ctrl+U.

Messages that relate to each other are listed together, in a hierarchy called a *thread*. To view hidden messages in a thread, click the plus sign in front of the lead message for that topic. To hide the messages again, click the minus sign that appears.

POSTING A MESSAGE

When posting a message, you have two choices: You can either reply to an existing message, or you can create a message with a new topic and post it. To create a message on a new topic, follow these steps:

1. Select the newsgroup you want to post a message to.

2. Click the Compose Message button.

3. Type a Subject.

4. Type your message in the large text box.

5. Click the Post Message button.

 Post to Several Newsgroups To post this same message to additional newsgroups, open the Tools menu and choose Select Newsgroups. Select the newsgroups you want to add and click Add. When you're through, click OK.

To comment on an existing message, follow these steps:

1. Select the message to which you want to reply.

2. Click the Reply to Group button.

 Respond Privately If you want to send a private message to the author of a newsgroup posting rather than posting your reply publicly, click Reply to Author instead.

---

3. Type your message in the large text box.

4. Click Post Message.

Wrong Message! If you want to cancel your posting after you've sent it, select the message, open the Compose menu, and select Cancel Message. Of course, if someone has already downloaded your message, this command won't remove the message from that person's system.

In this lesson, you learned how to subscribe to newsgroups and post messages. In the next lesson, you'll learn how to access files on a network.

USING NETWORK NEIGHBORHOOD

In this lesson, you'll learn how to access files and folders on your company's network.

WHAT IS A NETWORK?

A *network* is a collection of interconnected computers. Your computer might be part of a network, especially if you work for a large corporation. A network has *servers* and *clients*. A server shares a resource, such as a hard disk, a printer, or an application. A server can also provide a service, such as email handling. A client *uses* those resources.

On the network, your computer plays the role of the client, accessing the shared resources you need. However, with Windows 98, your PC can also play the role of a server, sharing the folders and files you designate with your coworkers.

 System Administrator The system administrator is the person who oversees the network's setup and operation. The system administrator adds and deletes users from the network, controls their access, performs network system updates, and troubleshoots problems.

USING A USER NAME AND PASSWORD

To gain access to the network's resources, you must log on. Logging on is a process that identifies you and your computer to the network through the use of a user name and password.

After learning your identity, the network determines which resources you have permission to access.

Your network's system administrator gives you your user name and password. Keep them in a safe place, because you won't be able to log onto your computer without them.

Accessing Shared Resources

You access the network's shared resources through the Network Neighborhood. Follow these steps:

1. Click (or double-click) the Network Neighborhood icon that appears on the Desktop, or click Network Neighborhood in the Explorer folder list. You can also select Network Neighborhood from the Address list in My Computer. You will see a list of servers available to you.

2. Besides the servers, you also can click or (double-click) the Entire Network icon. The workgroups on the network appear in the list. All servers are grouped into named workgroups for easier separation of departments. Many times there will be only a single workgroup.

3. Click (or double-click) on a specific workgroup. The servers on that workgroup appear in the listing.

4. To view the contents of a particular server, click (or double-click) it. You'll see the shared folders and printers attached to the network on the server. See Figure 28.1.

 No Access? If you have trouble accessing the files on a server, see your system administrator. The server might be down, or you might not have the necessary permission to use this particular resource.

Shared folder

Network printer

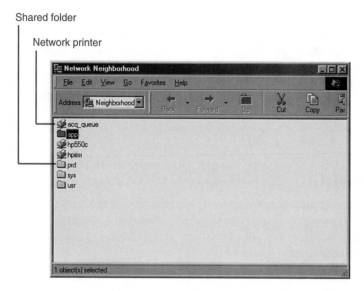

FIGURE 28.1   Using files on the network is similar to using them on your own computer.

5. From here, viewing files and folders is similar to using Explorer or My Computer. To view the files in a folder, click (or double-click) it. You can select files and copy them to your system if you like, but you probably won't have the access level necessary to delete network files unless you created them yourself.

6. To start a program located on the network, click (or double-click) its startup file. You can drag the startup file to your computer to create a shortcut to the program, giving you quicker access.

7. If you click (or double-click) a printer icon and that printer isn't yet set up for use on your computer, the Add Printer Wizard appears. Follow the steps to install the printer on your system. (You will need the Windows 98 installation disks for this task.)

Locating a Resource   You can use the Find command to locate a file, folder, or server on the network if you know its name. Click Start, select Find, and then select either Files and Folders or Computer. Type the name of the resource you want to locate, select Network Neighborhood, and click OK.

SHARING YOUR RESOURCES

You can share your computer's resources with others on the network if you like. When you share a resource, you determine the level of access you want to provide, and to whom. There are three levels of access:

Read Only   Users can view the contents of a file, but they can't change its data.

Full Access   Users can view and change the contents of a file.

Custom   A user's access level depends on his or her password.

If you are on a corporate LAN, you will likely be able to select specific access levels on a per-user basis, and that's what this section assumes. If you are not set up for this, you will only be able to specify a general read-only and full acess password on a per-resource basis.

To share a folder on the network, follow these steps:

1. Select the folder you want to share.

2. Open the File menu and select Sharing.

Select a user from this list   Click an access level

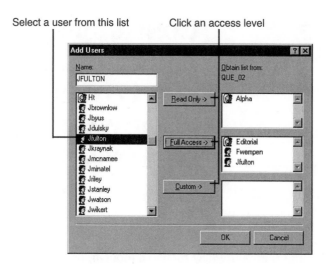

3. Click Shared As to enable sharing, and then click Add. The Add Users dialog box, shown in Figure 28.2, appears.

FIGURE 28.2   Selecting users to share with.

4. Select a user from the list on the left, and then click the button that describes the type of access level you want to assign. Repeat for additional users. To allow open access to the folder, select The world. Click OK.

5. If you're connected to the Internet through your company's network, you can share your folder on the Web. Click Web Sharing.

6. To share the contents of the folder for viewing, select Share folder for HTTP. To share the contents of the folder for downloading or uploading, select Share folder for FTP. Click OK.

7. Click OK. The folder appears in Explorer or My Computer with a shared icon (a hand holding a folder).

In this lesson, you learned how to access resources on the network. You also learned how to share your own resources.

CONFIGURING THE MODEM AND OTHER HARDWARE SETTINGS

When you first install Windows 98, it checks your system for hardware and configures it for use. However, if you upgrade your hardware or add something new such as a modem, printer, or tape backup, you'll need to configure it for use under Windows 98. In this appendix, you'll learn how to do just that.

CONFIGURING THE MODEM

You might use a modem to connect to the Internet or to an online service. You might also use a modem to connect from home to your office network.

ADDING A MODEM

Adding a new modem to your computer is fairly painless. But before you begin, make sure that your modem is on—if it's an external modem. If you use an internal modem, it's turned on when you turn on your PC.

To configure the modem for use, follow these steps:

1. Click Start, select Settings, and select Control Panel.

2. Click (or double-click) the Modems icon. The Modems Properties dialog box appears.

3. Click Add.

4. Turn on your modem and click Next >. Windows 98 will search for your modem.

5. Windows displays the name of your modem. If it's incorrect, you can click Change to display a list from which you can select. If Windows doesn't detect your modem, click Next > to display the modem list. After you've selected a correct modem name, click Next >.

 My Modem Isn't Listed!   If you can't locate your modem in the list, click Have Disk and use your modem's installation disk to install it.

6. Select the COM port for your modem, and click Next >.

 COM Port   Short for communications port, this is the port through which your computer communicates with serial devices such as a modem or a serial mouse.

7. Click Finish to add the modem.

8. You're returned to the Modems Properties dialog box. Click OK.

MODIFYING DIALING PROPERTIES

Once your modem is installed, you'll want to view the dialing properties and make any necessary changes. Follow these steps:

1. In the Modems Properties dialog box, click Dialing Properties. The Dialing Properties dialog box appears, as shown in Figure A.1.

2. Select your country and enter your area code.

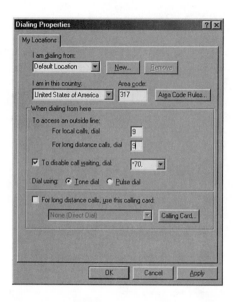

FIGURE A.1   Setting up your modem's properties.

3. If you need to dial 9 or some other number to get an out-side line, enter that number in the text boxes provided.

4. If you use call waiting, you'll want to disable it so that the modem won't try to answer an incoming call when you're online. Select the To disable call waiting, dial op-tion, and select the appropriate code for your area from the drop-down list.

5. Select Tone dial or Pulse dial (rotary dial).

6. If you use a calling card to charge long-distance phone calls, enter that information as well. Select the calling card option, and choose your card carrier from the drop-down list. Enter your card number by clicking the Calling Card button.

7. Click OK.

ADDING OTHER NEW HARDWARE

When you upgrade existing hardware or add new hardware, you should follow these steps to configure it:

1. Click Start, select Settings, and select Control Panel.

2. Click (or double-click) the Add New Hardware icon.

3. The Welcome box appears. Click Next >.

4. Click Next >. Windows checks your system for the new hardware.

5. Windows displays the name of the new hardware. Select the device from the list and click Next >. (If the device isn't listed, select the No option before clicking Next >, and Windows will search again.)

6. Click Finish.

CHANGING THE PROPERTIES OF AN OBJECT

Every object under Windows 98 has its own properties—from folders to files to applications. These properties tell you what the object is and what it can do. You can view these properties at any time and change them as needed. Follow these steps:

1. Right-click the icon for the object, or right-click its folder or filename.

2. Select Properties from the shortcut menu that appears. The Properties dialog box, shown in Figure A.2, appears. Each Properties dialog box contains tabs that are unique to that object.

3. Click the tab that contains the properties you want to view or change.

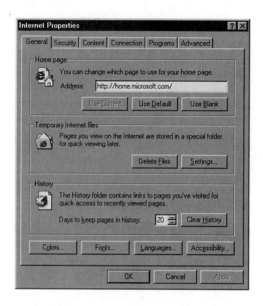

FIGURE A.2   A typical Properties dialog box.

4. Change whatever options you need to (you might need to consult the hardware manual), and then click Apply (if this button is provided in that particular Properties dialog box) to test your changes. Click OK when you're through.

Configuring for the Internet or an Online Service

Before you can begin using the Internet or an online service, you must configure your modem. Then you must configure the software that connects you to the service. Windows 98 comes with most of what you'll need to accomplish these tasks. If you need help configuring your modem, see Appendix A, "Configuring the Modem and Other Hardware Settings." In this appendix, you'll learn how to configure your system to connect to the Internet or to any of the more popular online services.

Using the Internet Connection Wizard

To help you configure your system for the Internet, Windows has supplied the Internet Connection Wizard. Follow these steps:

1. Double-click the Connect to the Internet icon on the Desktop, or click Start, and then select Programs | Internet Explorer | Connection Wizard.

2. The Welcome screen appears. Select the option you desire and click Next >:

   I want to sign up and configure my computer for a new Internet account   Choose this option if you haven't yet found an Internet service provider. Windows will help you locate a national provider that services your area code.

I have an existing Internet account through my phone line or a local area network (LAN).Help me set up my computer to connect to this Internet account   Choose this option if you have a local Internet provider you'd like to use.

My computer is already set up for the Internet. Do not show this wizard again   Select this option only if you've upgraded from a previous version of Windows and you've already set up your Internet connection.

SELECTING AN INTERNET SERVICE PROVIDER

If you selected I want to sign up and configure my computer for a new Internet account in step 3, continue by following these steps:

1. Click Next > to continue. The Wizard connects to Microsoft's Referral Service.

2. A list of national service providers in your area appears. To find out more about a particular provider, click on it. To sign up with that provider, select it from the list and click Next >, and then click Sign Me Up.

3. Enter the necessary information that's needed to sign up with your selected provider, and click Next >.

4. You might see a security alert, warning you that you're about to send information over the Internet. Click OK to continue.

5. You're connected to the Internet provider you selected. Follow the onscreen prompts to complete your installation.

USING YOUR OWN SERVICE PROVIDER

If you selected I have an existing Internet account through my phone line or a local area network (LAN). Help me set up my computer to connect to this Internet account in step 3, continue by following these steps:

1. Select whether you want to connect using a modem or through your company's network. Click Next >. If you're connecting through a modem, continue to step 2. Otherwise, follow these additional steps:

   Select Connect using my local area network (LAN) and click Next >. Then select whether your network uses a proxy server. Click Next >. If you're using proxy servers, enter their names, click Next >, and enter any exceptions (addresses that can bypass the proxy servers). Click Next >. Then skip to step 6.

2. Select Create a new dial-up connection and click Next >. Enter your service provider's phone number. Click Next >.

3. Type the user name and password you use to connect to your service provider. Click Next >.

4. Choose whether you want to change the advanced dial-up settings. These include using a SLIP connection, logging on manually or using a log-in script, and/or entering a specific IP and DNS address to connect to. Your service provider will tell you if you need to set up any of these options. If you do, click Yes and follow the prompts. Otherwise, select No and click Next > to continue.

5. Type a name for your dial-up connection file, such as Connection to Indy Net. Click Next >.

6. Click Yes to set up your email account, then click Next >. Click Create a new Internet mail account and click Next >.

7. Enter the name you want to appear on your email correspondence. Click Next >.

8. Enter your email address. Click Next >.

9. Select your email server type, and then enter the address of the incoming and outgoing mail servers. Click Next >.

10. Enter your email log-in name and password. Click Next >.

11. Type a name for your email connection file, such as IndyNet Mail. Click Next >.

12. Click Yes to set up your news server information now. The news server provides access to Internet newsgroups, as described in Lesson 27, "Using Outlook Express News." Click Next >. Click Create a new Internet news account and click Next >.

13. Enter the name you want to appear on your newsgroup postings. Click Next >.

14. Enter the email address to which you want people to re-ply to your newsgroup postings. Click Next >.

15. Enter the address of your newsgroup server. Click Next >.

16. Enter a name for the newsgroup connection file, such as **IndyNet News**. Click Next >.

17. Click Yes and follow the onscreen prompts to set up a new directory service. You might need to do this if your company's intranet provides an address book/directory service for your use. However, in most cases, you *will not* need to do this, because Windows already provides access to the major directory services, such as InfoSpace, Bigfoot, and Four11. In that case, click No. Click Next >.

18. Click Finish. You're through configuring your dial-up connection.

Using an Existing Connection

If you selected My computer is already set up for the Internet. Do not show this wizard again, you're done!

CONNECTING TO AN ONLINE SERVICE

An online service is a private service that restricts the use of its information to its members only. You can choose from many online services, including America Online, AT&T WorldNet, CompuServe, Prodigy, or the Microsoft Network.

Windows 98 provides an easy method for signing up for any of these services. Most of them even let you sign up for a short period of time as a trial. Follow these steps:

1. Click Start, select Programs, and select Online Services.

2. Select the online service you want to use.

3. Each service has a different setup program. You might be asked to insert the Windows installation diskettes to continue. Follow the onscreen prompts.

INDEX

G